CRYPTOCURRENCIES

THE MONEY OF THE FUTURE

MARCUS LISBOA

Cryptocurrencies: the money of the future
How Virtual Currency technology can change business
and the world in this new Crypto Digital Economy

2nd Edition
Marcus Lisboa, 2020
Miami – EUA

Edition and Revision:
Suellen de Araujo Costa
Layout, Graphic Design:
Marcus V. P. Alcântara
Cover:
Jonatas Santos
Editorial Coordination:
Nilce Sousa
English Edition:
Bianca E. Menezes Alves

Co-Authoring Chapter Blockchain on Environment and Agribusiness:
Cel Clyson Oliveira (Amazonas Coin)
Co-Authoring Chapter Crypto Trade:
Antônio Neto Ais
Co-Authoring Chapter Blockchain and Mining PoC and PoP:
Hugo Luigi
Collaborators:
Alexandre Nakatani, Paulo Lam, Sergio Magrini. Rafael Barbalho, Filipe Ferreira, Rodrigo Freitas, Danilo de Falco, Matheus Pagani, Allan Salvatierra e Robson Cocino

Organization:**Cevi Produções**
CNPJ 07.856.521/0001-94
Caldas Novas, Goiás - Brasil
Instagram: **@editoracevi**
ceviproducoes@gmail.com

L769c Lisboa, Marcus
    Cryptocurrencies the future of money / Marcus Lisboa. – 2. ed. – Caldas Novas-GO : CEVI, 2020.
    202 p. ; 21 cm.

    ISBN: 978-65-5642-029-5

1. Cryptocurrencies. 2. Blockchain. 3. Bitcoin. 4. Business. 5. Money Electronic. 6. Electronic funds transfers. 7. Innovations Technological. I. Maldonado, Jose. II. Luigi, Hugo. III. Título.
CDU: 658.8-52

Catalogação na publicação por: Onélia Silva Guimarães CRB-14/071

This is the first book in a series composed of three titles: "Cryptocurrencies: The Money of the Future", "The four types of transformative intelligence: Intelligences Applied to Christian Transformation in the Digital Age" and "The power of vision with a purpose: How Disruptive Technologies can transform and impact your life and the world."

This sequence entitled "Series: Digital Economy", seeks to explain complex themes, such as disruptive technologies, the new financial model brought by the emergence of virtual currencies, and especially, to show you how we can connect to these issues so present nowadays, to experience the breadth of its benefits, managing its use and serving the purpose and vision intended for us.

My wish is that you open yourself up to discover this relevant content, and allow yourself to have a new vision about the economy and its role within it, becoming a transforming agent in the environment where you live.

Acknowledgments

My especial thanks to Paula Vaz, Robson Silva, Marselha Samora, Harlisson Charley, Alexandre Hilgert and Alexandre Salgado, Carlos Guerreiro, Fabio Reis, Rubens Lemos, Romulo Souto, Pastor Carlos Almeida, Pastor Meire, Pastor Sidnei Borges, Pastor Eliane Pereira, Pastor Jean Kleber, Pastor Glabson, Pastor Joseph Maluta, Bishop JB Carvalho, Bishop Dirce Carvalho and Thomas Carter.

Dedication

would like to dedicate this work to my parents (*in Memorium*) Alfredo Almeida and Irene Lisboa, to my brothers Sérgio Luis, Carlos Alberto, Paulo César and Luis Cláudio, to my children Marcus Jr., Debora Regina, Jessyca Cristina, Priscila Maria, Andressa Santos, and Vinicius Galvão, to my beloved wife and companion Silvania Cristina Viegas, to my stepchildren, Junior, Moacir Neto, and Silveria Viegas, to my brothers-in-law, sisters-in-law, grandchildren and to all my nephews and friends.

About The Author

Marcus Lisboa, Systems and O&M Analyst, Cryptographer, Specialist in Public Interest Politics and Public Politics and Government Manager, Specialist in Disruptive Technologies, with International Certification in Digital Transformation & Blockchain, Founder of the Eco-System and Proof of Consensus called Proof of Participation – PoP (Blockchain Permitted), Blockchain enthusiast based on Proof of Consensus – PoC – Proof of Capacity, author of the following titles: Crypto Currencies – The Money of the Future; The Power of Vision with Purpose, and The Four Transformative Intelligences. Founding President of the National Institute of Public Politics Excellence – INEPP, Editor-in-Chief of the WikiCryptoMarket. com Blog, Creator of the Public Interest –

IP Channel, and member of the Council of Presidents of the Christian Center for Public Life – CCPL, known in Brazil as Conservative Christian Organization, with headquarters in Washington and national headquarters in Brasília – Distrito Federal, and creator of the professional education portal in the area of Crypto Assets, Crypto Trader and Crypto-Economy www.cryptotech.com.br.

Summary

Introduction

Technology has evolved so rapidly in the past century that most people cannot keep pace with it. We have already heard some people say: "Oh, I'm getting old, I think I'll be left behind" solely because they don't understand what these essential innovations have to offer in the future. However, the correct knowledge of how these technologies can change our lives, our way of relating to the world, with people and even our professions in the near future, shows us how fundamental it is to us.

By neglecting to predict how these new technologies would change the course of the market so drastically, for example, large companies "stopped in time" and went bankrupt, some even becoming completely obsolete.

An example of this is Kodak, which was a company that quickly dominated its segments. To give you an idea, in the United States alone, in 1976, Kodak sold 85% of cameras and 90% of films. Worldwide, the percentages were over 50%. The big problem is that the company did not join the digital market in time, and suffered a crisis so devastating that it had to declare bankruptcy in 2012, despite having continued activities in a much-reduced proportion. First, digital cameras and, subsequently, the advancement and sophistication of smartphones, completely dominated this market.

If you were born in the '90s or before, you could still remember the fax machine, the vinyl record, the tape player, the telegram, the k7 tape, and other devices that have become archaic. The revolution in digital technology and telecommunications was the starting point of the great break with the old way of communicating, and also of entertainment.

Even in countries that are lagging behind, such as Nepal, for example, it is not possible to pay bills via the banking system. Before the great technological advancement of the financial system, we can remember a not so distant past in which the bills were paid only at banks and receipts recorded in booklets. There were no credit or debit cards.

Faced with a scenario of massive and frantic transformation, I desire to open to the reader, a window to the great innovation in the financial market that is about to change the course of monetary relations even more in the coming years. Yes, that's right, in a few years it may be that you no longer have a bank account like you do today.

Similar to the shift from long lines at cashiers to paying bills via online banking, it may be that the way we buy, sell, store and invest our money today be replaced by a more straightforward, more productive, and globalized model.

Cryptocurrency technology has come to stay, decentralize, and revolutionize financial relationships between individuals, companies, organizations, and countries. It has been proven that it is not just a speculative bubble, but the money of the future.

Before understanding this technology that will break with the configuration and functioning of the current financial and monetary system, I would like to give a brief presentation on the basic concept that amplifies our field of understanding on the subject. This technology is not only designed as an innovation that can make our lives easier, but it is something that will have a much more profound impact.

But before anything, we cannot correctly speak of **cryptocurrencies** (or **"Blockchain"** technology), their impact, and relevance, without first discerning an essential term: the concept of **Disruptive Technology**.

Chapter 1

What is Disruptive Technology and its effects

The term "Disruptive Technology" first appeared in a 1995 article called Disruptive Technologies: Catching the Wave. Later on, Harvard author and Professor Clayton Christensen described this theory in a better way in his books, The Innovator's Dilemma and The Innovator's Solution.

He was inspired by the concept of "creative destruction" coined by Austrian economist Joseph Schumpeter in 1939 to explain business cycles. According to him, capitalism works in cycles, and each new revolution (industrial or technological) completes a cycle that destroys the previous market and starts a new one.

Disruptive technology or **disruptive innovation** is a term that describes the technological innovation of products or services, with "disruptive" characteristics, instead of evolutionary ones. That is, they break with the standards, models, or technologies already established in the market.

As we saw in the Kodak example, the market for analog cameras had been swallowed up by the new market for digital cameras and smartphones.

The term means that which "interrupts the normal course" and creates a discontinuity and is, therefore, transformative or revolutionary.

The term became popular among young entrepreneurs in Silicon Valley and was appropriated by marketing and advertising strategies. It is currently used to promote products or services that are considered innovative in a variety of ways.

Disruptive or revolutionary inventions are a minority when compared to other types of innovations introduced into the market. They cannot be confused with a simple innovation or with the improvement of existing technologies - these are prevalent processes in terms of technological development.

I'll list here 7 (seven) areas of technology that will have a massive potential impact over the next 10 (ten) years, that is, potentially disruptive technologies. Each of these areas has different applications. Let's see below:

01. Internet of Things (IoT): It is all the produced technology that can send and receive data through the network. The internet of things connects devices and vehicles using electronic sensors and the internet.

It is any remote system used by different electronic equipment, with an unlimited application, from an advanced Pentagon security system to a TV that connects to the internet.

We already see the concept, for example, of "smart home", in which the use of the network allows the control of many things, such as lighting, temperature, activation of household appliances like programming the toaster to work when you usually wake up, or the coffee maker, to brew a cup of coffee for when you are coming home. There are numerous possibilities for integration with systems and devices available in the market, and many others are under development.

All of this is related to the Internet of Things movement, which aims to connect everyday items to the Internet, to collect information in real-time, and to help to make people's lives better.

Imagine this in security systems, sensors that pick up and process information from your body to analyze your health, clothes that detect and control your body temperature, smart glasses for video calls, and the list goes on. It is estimated that by 2020, 20 billion devices will be connected to the network.

02. Artificial Intelligence (AI): It is a branch of computer science that proposes to develop devices that simulate the human capacity to reason, perceive, make decisions, and solve problems. In short, the ability to be intelligent. The applications are also diverse. We have seen a growing use of AI in automated customer service, advertising, and marketing systems (robots), data processing, increasing usage of "interacting robots" in vehicles and smartphones.

03. Advanced Robotics: It is the technology that enables the replacement of humans by robots in the performance of common or more advanced tasks. Mechanization of production processes by robots, humanoid prototypes with productive capacity. In medicine, the precision of robots has been replacing medical fallibility in many situations, such as risky surgeries. This technology is also responsible for high-performance prostheses capable of replacing parts of the human body, performing tasks as well as natural ones. There are even ongoing creations of robots that aim to replace human relationships.

04. New Generation Sequencing: Genetic technology has advanced exponentially. The DNA molecule is composed of nucleotides linked in specific and unique combinations that can be identified by the sequencing methodology. However, it was from 2005 that the "new generation sequencing" technology (genome project) allowed a new approach to large-scale **sequencing**. It has allowed the development of possible vaccines, therapies, and treatments for diseases not yet curable, such as cancer, HIV, diabetes, and congenital anomalies.

05. Alternative Energy: The generation of energy from renewable sources such as solar and wind is undoubtedly innovative, especially when compared to traditional energy sources. According to experts, renewable energy will globally minimize climate change and pollution. Renewable energy includes technological inventions such as wind turbines, photovoltaic cells, concentrated solar power, geothermal energy, ocean wave energy, among others. That is another excellent example of disruptive technology that will accelerate sustainable development.

06. Blockchain Technology: This is a "decentralized accounting" technology that makes Bitcoin, Stellar (Lumens), Ethereum, and hundreds of other digital currencies possible, providing a record of transactions and confirming who has what at any time. Sophisticated cryptographic processes ensure its security. The immediate impact of blockchain technology may not be apparent to the non-technological eye, but it will certainly improve existing systems within society as a whole.

07. Quantum Technology: This is a technology and a new field of physics and engineering, which gives some of the strange characteristics of quantum mechanics, especially quantum entanglement and, more recently, quantum tunneling practical applications such as quantum computing, quantum cryptography, quantum simulation, quantum metrology, the quantum sensor, and the quantum image.

The field of quantum technology has benefited enormously from ideas coming from the field of quantum informatics, particularly quantum computing. Different areas of quantum physics, such as quantum optics, atomic optics, quantum electronics, and non-mechanical quantum devices, have been unified in the search for the quantum computer and the quantum information theory table.

One can compare disruptive innovation, roughly speaking, to a paradigm shift: Thomas Kuhn already pointed out in the 1960s that ordinary science produces a series of concepts, ideas, revising old concepts and creating a favorable context for, at any given moment a scientific revolution may arise and rearticulate the field of knowledge.

In the case of technological innovations, there is a similar process. Technologies are continually being improved, new applications and new materials are emerging, and at a particular point, a company or entrepreneur reorganizes the elements and propose a different, simpler, and more efficient way of doing things, changing the way it was done until so.

Disruptive innovation is the phenomenon by which an innovation transforms an existing market or sector by introducing simplicity, convenience, and accessibility in companies where the complications and the high costs are the status quo. When a niche market is already out of date (or remains steady, without growth or innovation), and seems uninteresting or irrelevant, it is surprised by a new product or idea that completely reshapes the industry, which leads to disruptive innovation.

Chapter 2

Blockchain for beginners and enthusiasts

Now that we understand in more detail the background that makes up the development of disruptive technologies, we can better explore what Blockchain technology is and everything that derives from it.

First, we need to understand the difference between a **centralized system**, a **decentralized system,** and a **distributed system**.

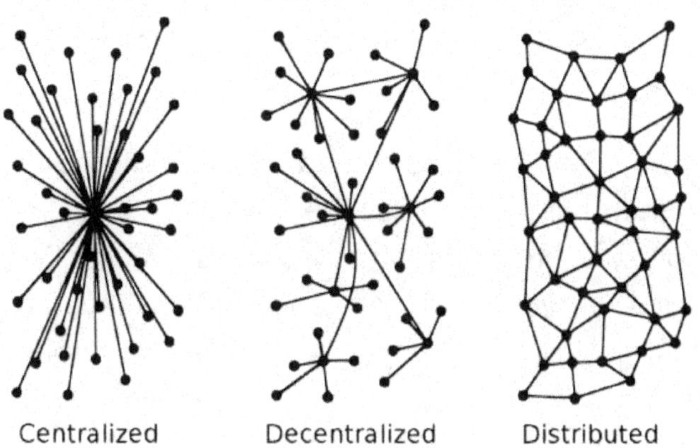

In the chart above, we see that in the **centralized system**, all parties involved are linked and depend entirely on a single point of convergence. In other words, for this system to work, there is an agent or individual who has complete access and control of everything. We can cite the bank as an example. If individual A wishes to make a payment or financial transfer for individual B, he must necessarily pass through the central point, which is the bank, and through it, carry out the transaction that guarantees the evidence of all the transactions. The bank is the record validator.

In the **decentralized system**, we see a more extensive network composed of several centralized networks. The small "nodes" of this network reveal centralized subnets. The network does not depend on a single server, but it shares the risk with several central nodes, each managing a limited amount of "endpoint" nodes.

On the other hand, in the **distributed system**, no individual or agent centralizes, controls, inspects and validates transactions, but everyone, all at once, can have this responsibility and capacity. If individual A makes a transfer to individual B, everyone in the system will be able to validate and attest that this actually happened.

Blockchain can take on both a decentralized and distributed architecture. At the end of 2008, Satoshi Nakamoto announced the development of a peer-to-peer **electronic money system** (money from the internet), that is, that would pass from one hand to another, from point to point directly, without an intermediary or centralizer.

This technology allowed the sharing of digital media files using a software program that searches for other computers connected to the same network to find the desired content. The nodes (peers) on these networks are end-user computers or distribution servers.

Until Satoshi's invention, the technology was being used to share books, music, movies, and games. Sharing a fully decentralized digital currency was a revolution.

The term blockchain means a "chain of blocks." Each block contains the history of certain financial transactions that took place. And the "hash" is the "name" that identifies each block. All blocks are linked and protected using cryptography[1]. Each block typically contains a hash pointer as a link to a previous block, a timestamp, and transaction data. By

---

1. Cryptography definition:1.It is a set of principles and techniques employed to encrypt writing, making it incomprehensible for those who do not have access to the combined conventions; cryptology.

2. In political, diplomatic, military, criminal operations, etc., codified modification of a text, to prevent its understanding by those who do not know its characters or conventions.

design, blockchains are inherently resistant to data modification.

It is an open and distributed book that can record transactions between two parties in an efficient, correct, and permanent way. For use as a distributed book, a blockchain is typically managed by a peer-to-peer network by collectively joining a protocol to validate new blocks.

Once recorded, the data in any given block cannot be changed retroactively without changing all subsequent blocks, which requires collusion of the most part of the network.

Blockchains are safe by design and are an example of a distributed computing system with a high tolerance for byzantine failures. The decentralized consensus was reached with a blockchain. It solves the problem of double-spending, without the need for a trusted authority or central server.

Blocking time is the average time it takes for the network to generate an extra block on the blockchain. Some blockchains create a new block every five seconds depending on the cryptocurrency. Upon completion of the block, the data included becomes verifiable. It is practically when the money transaction takes place; therefore, a shorter blocking time means faster transactions.

Bitcoin was the first cryptocurrency created, responsible for the spread of blockchain technology in the world.

Bitcoin and Ethereum are the two main currencies, representing hundreds of billions of dollars, which together represent more than 50% of the total market share of cryptocurrencies.

While the Bitcoin blockchain is used almost exclusively for operations within the digital currency BTC, the Ethereum blockchain is a more complex and even more audacious platform, whose purpose is to be used for the creation of smart contracts, creation of other currencies, and tokenization of assets. Today, there are already other Blockchain platforms that are also already entering this market of smart contracts and tokenization of digital assets.

The traditional stock market will be directly affected by this new technology that promises to simplify asset purchase and sale operations **worldwide, including new private and state digital asset exchange that are already being created.**

But before we proceed to analyze the differences between these two platforms, it is important to remember that the use of a blockchain network can assume different architectures, as shown in the figure.

The clearest example of a distributed network is the Bitcoin blockchain: anyone can download Bitcoin Core, become a node in the network, and have read and writing access to all blockchain records.

On the other hand, to manage a supply chain for a group of companies (such as Walmart, for example), or a group of banks that want to use blockchain to speed up their transactions (as in the R3 Consortium, for example), data will not be public, and not everyone will have the right to write in the distributed database. So, as we have seen, a system with centralized subnets is necessary. Example: Blockchain with proof of Consensus PoP – Proof of Participation.

And some projects fit within the two architectures, in which the reading can be public and the writing restricted, or vice versa. The important thing is to understand two aspects of the different blockchain applications:

· Not all networks need to be public and open like Bitcoin.

· There are applications where the characteristic anonymity of Bitcoin does not apply because when we imagine a blockchain between banks, it is evident that the identity of the participants of the transactions is fundamental; therein comes the Permitted architecture.

Chapter 3

The evolution of the monetary experience

We are entering a more technical path. A historical explanation of monetary developments may help us understand in a broader view, the new courses that await us in the near future. In this chapter, we'll look at how trading, buying, and selling relationships have evolved into the complex and diverse forms of today's financial market.

The current currency and revolutionary cryptocurrencies are the results of the evolutionary process of human relations. Follow the development of monetary affairs, from bartering to digital currencies bellow:

FROM BARTERING TO PAPER CURRENCY

(From Prehistory to Antiquity):

Barter: the exchange of the surplus between people, without the concern of the equivalence of value. The first human groups, nomads in general, did not know the currency and used direct exchanges of objects (called bartering) when they wanted something they did not have. Some even felt at a loss in specific trades.

Product currency (merchandise – currency): more useful products had more value. However, there was a problem: they were not fractional; they were perishable, etc. Examples of currency products:

• Salt: where the term "salary" originates.

• Cattle: from which came the notion of the Treasury Department, known as "Farming Ministry" in Brazil.

• Sugar; cocoa; pau-brazil (redwood); tobacco etc.

Metal currency: Precious metals started to have more general acceptance and a more limited offer, which guaranteed them a stable and high price. Moreover, they did not wear out, were easily recognizable, divisible, and light. However, there was always the problem of weighing.

Monetary currency: the first records of the use of metallic coins date from Seventh Century BC., when they were minted in Lydia, the kingdom of Asia Minor, and also in the region of the Peloponnese, at the south of Greece.

FROM PAPER CURRENCY TO CRYPTOCURRENCY

(Middle Ages to today)

Historically, technology has changed the way we relate to money, generating less reliance on banknotes through digitalization, or even the innovative virtual economic system.

Paper Currency - China, 960 AD: Paper money came into the scene to solve the inconveniences of the metal coin (weight, risk of theft), although they were backed by it. Then, there were the certificates of deposit issued by houses of custody in exchange for the precious metals deposited there. Later they evolved into other types not fully supported.

• Analogous to the current model that lasted until the 14th century.

• Resurges in the 17th century in Sweden.

• Brazil: emerges in 1810, written by hand and called "banknotes."

Banking currency: created by commercial banks, this currency corresponds to all demand and short-term deposits, and is done through checks or money orders - instruments used to transfer and move them. Currently, the two forms of currency used are fiduciary and bank, which has only exchange value.

Credit cards: emerged in 1920 in the USA, made initially of cardboard paper.

• 1920: They were restricted to companies: given to loyal customers who were able to pay bills on time. Similar to the "booklets."

• 1950: Creation of the Diners Club - restricted to 200 users considered important, accepted in only 27 restaurants.

• 1955: Diners become plastic. They are still using the founding name to this day.

• 1958: American Express created their card, but it was in 1966 that BankAmerican Service Corporation created the successful BankAmericard

card. It was accepted in more than 12 million establishments, and, shortly after that, it was renamed to what we currently know as Visa. In the same year, the Master Charge was created, which later became MasterCard.

Automated Teller Machine - ATM (1983)

Online transactions:

- 1979: Created for a restricted market.

- 1990: Became popular throughout the world.

- 1995: Began its popularization in Brazil.

Smartphone Revolution: 2000s - the bank in one touch; the world in our hands.

In 2008, at the height of the American crisis that led to the collapse of several financial institutions, Satoshi Nakamoto appeared in online discussions using anonymizing programs from his account and inviting volunteers to help develop his project in the Cryptography Mailing discussion group. Satoshi Nakamoto was, therefore, the codename responsible for publishing the article with the central idea of the BITCOIN protocol (BTC) in 2009.

Open source allowed the developer community to contribute to the improvement of the protocol. The real identity of the programmer, who identified himself as a 38-year-old Japanese man, and could write in British and American English without fail, was never discovered. After his involvement with the project came to an end in 2010, he simply disappeared, claiming that he had "gone to find new things."

There are some speculations about his true identity, including:

• Gavin Andresen: chief developer of Bitcoin Foundation (founded in 2011).

• Shinichi Mochizuki: an influential Japanese mathematician known for solving one of the most complex problems in mathematics, the ABC conjecture.

• A pseudonym: used by a group of programmers to protect themselves. In Japanese, the translation of the pseudonym would be "clear thinking within the foundation" (Satoshi = "clear or wise thinking", Naka = "inside", Moto = "foundation").

Anyway, Nakamoto's identity is of little relevance to the development of Bitcoin, since his system does not depend on any particular person or organization. What matters is that the currency appears to be a concrete solution for the future, with a market already moving more than 100 billion dollars.

An interesting curiosity: China intends to trade only with digital currencies by 2030. In other words, the one responsible for creating paper money wants to be the first to extinguish it!

Bitcoin, as we already know, is a point-to-point electronic money system that does not depend on any central authority to function. Unlike fiduciary currency that is controlled and issued by a central bank, bitcoin units are issued through a process known as "mining."

Mining consists of computers vying to solve a mathematical problem whose solution provides network security and the validity of the record of your transactions. Currently, competing for this reward requires a lot of computing power and specialized hardware, known as Application-Specific Integrated Circuit (ASIC).

In order to encourage communities to spend considerable sums on energy, and the purchase of increasingly sophisticated hardware, each block contains two types of rewards: newly created bitcoins (new bitcoins are issued at a fixed and decreasing rate limited to 21 million units) and fees (small fees) charged to validate the network – community transactions.

The rewards are sent to the miner or the group of miners (as usually occurs and whose process is called mining pool), which successfully solves the mathematical problem. The person responsible for the solution also gains the right to register his block in the chain.

The Bitcoin Protocol states that every 10 minutes, someone will be able to solve this problem and can claim their reward. In other words, no matter how many miners are working on the network, someone will always be successful every 10 minutes and can claim their compensation. That is due to the dynamic and automatic adjustment of the network. Every 2,106 blocks, the equation resets the target of difficulty, measuring the time it took to find the last 2,106 blocks.

Another phenomenon that should help the expansion of the Crypto Assets would be the new Decentralized Exchange Technologies, known in the market as DEX, starting with one of the market leaders, Binance, which follows a predominant centralized hybrid model, now decentralized, but still nascent. However, this is a natural tendency for the exchange market from 2021, which genuinely follows the logic of crypto assets, which came to be disruptive, decentralized, and distributed. Until now, at least, its market had concentrating characteristics and centralized database, which is nonsense when we think about the nature and premise of Blockchain, whether in decentralized and / or distributed open architecture, or permitted and equally decentralized architecture.

The increase in the community of the digital currency market encouraged the emergence of numerous companies specializing in providing services to this public:

• Exchange houses, brokerage houses;

• Digital Wallets and Digital Custody Houses;

• ATM companies;

• Consulting services;

• Information exchange channels;

• Manufacture of supercomputers;

We cannot ignore, however, the similar interest of criminals, who see an opening for financial crimes in the anonymity, lack of control, global aspect, and agility. An example of this was the case of the Silk Road website.

For a long time, no one knew who was (or were, since it could be a single name used by more than one person) Dread Pirate Roberts. All we knew was that he was the owner of Silk Road, a website that sells (obviously illegal) drugs that operated on the deep web and made transactions using Bitcoins, to ensure anonymity, for both the buyer and the seller. But today, DPR had its identity revealed by the FBI: Dread Pirate Roberts was the pseudonym used by Ross Ulbricht to remain anonymous on the internet. And, of course, he was arrested.

The anonymity worked for two years; Silk Road, the most extensive website of its kind, was open in 2011. It is estimated that it has handled more than $ 1.3 billion in Bitcoins. When it was closed in 2013, it led to a currency drop of 22%. Most applications request one or no ID to open a virtual wallet. Also, they use anonymizing software such as TOR, for example, and others.

CHINA ANNOUNCING ITS STATE CRYPTO e-RMB

We recently saw China announce its 100% Legal Block Fashion project on Blockchain permitted, using already existing hybrid Blockchain solutions, initiating the previously announced process of competing with the USD in the world economy, starting the new cycle of a new 100% digital economy and putting on an accelerated course.

China has an ambitious and dangerous project to assume the dominance of this new global digital financial system with its own currency in Blockchain, which would force countries with significant export dependencies of their production to China to adopt their Digital Currency in Blockchain, replacing the monetary reference established as a standard and value reserve, which was the dollarization of the World Economy until that moment.

That will precipitate Blockchain projects in other countries such as the USA, Europe, Latin America, and I believe that Brazil is one of the pioneers, as our Central Bank has been preparing for this moment and the Ministry of Economy has been giving clear signs that this is a path with no return; the Legal Course and Forced Course currency coexisting with private Crypto Assets like BTC, Libra, and other State Crypto Assets, in addition to AltCoins that are already positioned in the Coin Market Capital.

Chapter 4

Crypto-Economy and Digital and Financial Transformation

So far, we have seen the fundamentals for understanding crypto-economy: **Technological Disruption** and **Digital and Financial Transformation** with Blockchain Technology, and the history and impact of the first and most important **virtual** currency, Bitcoin. However, we need to understand that this technology and its ramifications overgrow. By the beginning of 2019, there were more than 1,195 digital currencies on the market, currently over 3,000 crypto assets, and increasing every year.

The profiles of the majority of the users who have launched themselves in this market are 32-year-old males, technology aficionados, and digital libertarian natives, but there is no final profile outlined. They aim for profit, political aspirations, anonymity, and decentralization.

Although it may still seem a bit confusing, we need to establish some conceptual differences between **virtual**, **digital**, and **cryptocurrency** or **crypto assets**. Although **virtual currency** is indistinctly referred to as

digital currency or **cryptocurrency / crypto assets**, there are some differences:

• **Digital currency** is every virtual currency that is electronically created and stored.

• **Every digital currency is a virtual currency**, but not every virtual currency is digital.

• **Cryptocurrency / Crypto Asset** is a subgroup of decentralized and / or distributed digital currencies, or in some cases, permitted and equally decentralized, but always encrypted.

• **Every Cryptocurrency / Crypto Asset** is a digital currency, but not every digital currency is a cryptocurrency / crypto asset.

A **cryptocurrency / crypto asset**, therefore, is a means of exchange using blockchain technology and cryptography to ensure the validity of transactions and the creation of new currency units. The first one was Bitcoin, and since then, many other cryptocurrencies have been created. More recently, there has been an explosion of many tokens that have been created based on the Ethereum protocol, especially after the massive Initial Coin Offering (**ICO**) wave that occurred in 2017. Currently, due to the failure of several

ICO-based projects, the market prefers to opt for a more conservative line called **STO**, Security Token Offering, with regulation and supervision by the authorities of the capital and investment market.

What is Ethereum? It is a protocol with the ability to execute pre-programmed contracts automatically. However, its applications are not limited to this. Its greatness lies in the capacity of its creators, especially Vitalik Buterin, to observe the characteristics of the Bitcoin protocol and to understand the depth of technology beyond the features already proposed and in existence. The creation of the Ethereum was intended further to deepen the impact of blockchain on everyday life.

The platform aims to create applications associated with blockchain, which run exactly as programmed. Ideally, there is no possibility of censorship, fraud, or interference from third parties. Also, it provides an ecosystem for developers to create decentralized applications that work on the protocol itself. Despite being a relatively new project, products with enormous potential to restructure society are already watched. These projects focus on the most diverse areas: ranging from online voting systems to fully decentralized and autonomous institutions.

Altcoin

The term altcoin has several similar definitions. Stephanie Yang of The Wall Street Journal defined altcoins as "alternative digital currencies," while Paul Vigna, also of The Wall Street Journal, described altcoins as "alternative versions of Bitcoin." Aaron Hankins of MarketWatch refers to any cryptocurrency other than Bitcoin as altcoins.

A decentralized cryptocurrency is produced collectively by a cryptocurrency system for a defined reason when the system is created and publicly available. In centralized banking or economic systems, such as the United States Federal Reserve System, boards of directors or governments control the money supply through the printing of fiduciary currency. However, corporations or governments cannot produce cryptocurrency units, and thus, have not yet provided support for other entities, banks, or corporations that hold assets measured through a decentralized cryptocurrency, or crypto assets, that are public or permitted.

There are hundreds of specifications on cryptocurrencies, the vast majority being similar and derived from the first decentralized currency implemented, the

Bitcoin. A community of miners maintains the security, integrity, and balance of records of a cryptocurrency system: members of the general public using their computers to help validate and time transactions, adding them to the record (blockchain) according to a defined timing scheme.

The security of cryptocurrency records is based on the assumption that most miners are honestly keeping the file, having a financial incentive to do so.

Most cryptocurrencies are designed to reduce the production of new currencies, thereby defining a maximum number of currency that will go into circulation. This imitates the scarcity (and value) of precious metals and avoids hyperinflation if compared to conventional currencies held by financial institutions or in the form of cash in hands.

Digital Wallets

Digital wallets have emerged to make more accessible the use of cryptocurrency, or crypto assets, public or permitted, and make their storage more secure. Unlike cash in a traditional bank account, where the account is associated with an account holder and an account number, cryptocurrencies, or crypto assets, do not necessarily need a similar structure to be stored.

Digital wallets function as an interface interacting with the blockchain. To send Bitcoins or any other type of digital currency to a digital wallet, a user signs the cryptocurrency with a private key to the wallet address. In order to be able to spend these currencies, the private key stored in the user's wallet must match the public address to which the cryptocurrency is assigned, and, if this match occurs, the cryptocurrency will be attached to the wallet. This transaction is registered on the blockchain.

Software-based digital crypto software wallets, for example, do not hold user information, ensuring anonymity. Usually, a user buys a virtual currency at an exchange (as if they were exchange houses of cryptocurrencies), like binance.com, poliniex.com, bitsblockchain.net, mercadobitcoin.com, novadex.com.br, and others, where the cryptocurrency is stored under exchange control. A disadvantage of this approach is that if this exchange is hacked, the funds will be lost, in addition to the control of the cryptocurrency being the exchange. So, it is essential to know how to choose the exchange that you will work with, and analyze its reputation and security aspects.

Another option would be to store the cryptocurrency in a software-based wallet, or hot wallets, which have internet access. The user provides the address for his digital wallet on the exchange, and their funds are transferred. In these wallets, the user's private keys, necessary to perform the cryptocurrency transactions, are not stored on the servers' wallet, but on the user's computer; soon, he has control of the cryptocurrency. Software-based digital crypto software wallets also conduct transactions and deal with the blockchain.

They can store a single type of cryptocurrencies, such as Coinwise, or several cryptocurrencies, such as Coinomi, however, the owner must take good care of his computer's security.

Another option is a hardware-based digital wallet, or cold storage, where a specific device stores the user's private keys. This device is connected to the computer that is connected to the Internet only when the user wants to perform a cryptocurrency transaction. After completing the transaction, the device is removed and kept off the internet, where it is not subject to attacks by hackers.

Software-based electronic wallets

Here we will deal with digital wallets that use software connected to the internet to carry out transactions. It may be software installed on the user's machine or a web page. These wallets can store only one type of cryptocurrency or be "multi-currency" (they store multiple cryptocurrencies). These wallets can carry out cryptocurrency transactions and deal directly with the blockchain. These wallets are subdivided into three types: **Desktop - Mobile – Web.**

- Desktop

A digital desktop wallet is a software downloaded and installed on the user's computer that is not accessible via the internet; that is, it can only be used on the computer where the software is installed. This software must have access to the internet to be able to enter the wallet and carry out cryptocurrency transactions. If the computer where the software is installed is attacked by malicious agents (hackers), the funds in the wallet will be compromised. An example of such a wallet is Electrum.

- Mobile

A digital mobile wallet is an app for smartphones running on iOS or Android. It has the advantage of portability and can be used anywhere with online access, enabling purchases in stores that accept cryptocurrency. Usually, they are more straightforward than desktop wallets, since the storage space of a mobile phone is smaller. An example of such a wallet is Mycelium.

- Web

An "online digital wallet" is stored in the cloud and is accessible from any device with the ability to connect to a web page. They are practical and straightforward to use, however, they store the user's private keys on the wallet's server, which means that the control of the funds is not directly with the user, making it more susceptible to hacker attacks or theft by the wallet itself. An example of this type of wallet, as we have already seen, is Coinwise.

A digital wallet that uses hardware

A hardware-based digital cryptocurrency wallet uses a physical device to ensure transaction security. This device is only connected to a computer connected to the internet to perform the cryptocurrency transaction and is withdrawn after the transaction.

One of the advantages of this type of wallet is that by staying out of the internet, the cryptocurrency remains more secure and less prone to attacks by hackers.

In some of these wallets, to perform the cryptocurrency transaction, the user is asked to press a button on the device. By storing your funds in this type of digital wallet, the user is protected from hacker attacks on exchanges. An example of this type of wallet is Trezor.

- **Other types of wallets**

There are also other types of cryptocurrency wallets. The term Brainwallet refers to the concept of memorizing, through the use of mnemonic phrases, Bitcoin private key addresses, which means it would be safe from hackers. However, if the person forgets it or somehow becomes incapacitated, the Bitcoins will be lost forever.

Another possible type of wallet is the physical, paper wallets, containing a QR Code, a public key, and a private key. If the wallet is stolen, the person who has that paper will be able to use the funds associated with the wallet.

- **Legality**

The legality of cryptocurrencies varies substantially from one country to another and is still undefined in many others. While some countries have explicitly authorized their use and exchange, such as Germany, others restricted or even banned them, such as Saudi Arabia. Similarly, various government agencies, departments, and courthouses have classified Bitcoins in different ways.

The Central Bank of China banned the use of Bitcoins by financial institutions in the country during a period of extremely rapid adoption in early 2014. In Russia, although cryptocurrencies are legal, it is illegal to purchase products with any currency other than the Russian Ruble. However, by the end of 2018, 14 countries had already developed projects ready to be able to launch their cryptocurrencies on the market, with state characteristics and quite distinct from the disruptive movement that the decentralized cryptocurrencies brought to the market.

Chapter 5

Smart Contracts and Asset Tokenization

Smart Contracts

A contract established between parties traditionally will always be liable not to be enforceable. Machines develop smart contracts. These machines will execute it in an impartial, free, and expert way and register in the network in an immutable and inviolable way. All the functions for which the Smart Contract is automatically programmed are guaranteed.

However, there are groups of companies that may not "trust" each other directly. But blockchain solves the problem of lack of trust in the corporate world. It works almost like insurance, through the development of decentralized applications.

– The following elements are part of a smart contract on the blockchain:

– The object of the contract (what).

– The digital signature of the participants of the contract (who).

–   Contract terms (how).

–   Decentralized, distributed platform.

A smart contract can be drawn up, for example, between components of a logistics chain so that as the assets move in that chain and each party fulfills its step in the process, the financial aspects are automatically executed (payments, transfers, etc.).

Smart contract applications have been increasingly common in voting systems, logistics, auctions, insurance, real estate buying / selling, music, among other businesses. Another sector in which these contracts can be used is the Public sector; as, for example, in the registration of automobiles, property, in the electoral registration, etc.

The author makes available to the smart contract market based on Open Source Blockchain, with Proof of Capacity – PoC, and another equally Native and Permitted blockchain called PoP – Proof of Participation.

Tokenization of Assets

Tokenization means turning a real asset into digital tokens, allowing these tokens to be traded (bought / sold), increasing the liquidity, and the potential market size for these assets. The best way to understand this logic is by using an example.

Consider a property as an asset, which, in our case, has a market value of $1 million US dollars. Now imagine that this property will be tokenized, and 20 tokens will be created, each equivalent to 5% of the property value. That way, you could own a part of the property, or for example, receive part of the income from rent, if that's the case. The market is much larger, as tokens can be traded just like any digital currency, anywhere in the world, 24 hours a day, uninterrupted.

The author also makes available for Tokenization of Digital assets a new Consensus proof, called PoP – Proof of Participation, with an auto generator of Tokens, to enable the tokenization of practically all types of real, physical, financial, real state, and patrimonial assets.

Digital Currencies of Legal Course or State Digital Currencies in Blockchain

Currently, some countries are already developing their cryptocurrency or crypto assets projects, using Permitted Blockchains technology, with centralized and some decentralized characteristics, but only two with distributed components; they are:

Current Public / Private Blockchain Projects and State Central Banks: United Arab Emirates, Japan, China, Australia, Switzerland, Canada, France, Bahamas, Sweden, Seborga, and the supra-territorial project called AFRA / SAPA / BCA. Other countries are already starting studies and implementations.

Chapter 6

How Digital Currencies will change business and the World

We have seen that several innovations and transformations have changed the history of the world, which at first nobody believed. And because of this disbelief, many people missed the train of history, not boarding at the right time, with the right innovation and in the appropriate market. And once they have missed this great opportunity, they can only observe the visionary people who boarded the locomotive while the doors were still open.

We have seen it with telecommunications, the internet, and the world of opportunities that they have opened up. Now, we are facing a new moment, which, similar to the innovations mentioned above, will completely revolutionize the market of digital finance, capital, investments, and applied technology, the crypto-economy.

The revolution that blockchain platforms brought to the market is already recognized as the most incredible and the safest technology ever developed by man in all time.

FINANCIAL MARKET

We are in the middle of a battle between the more "conservative" agents and the more "progressive" agents. The first will not give up the established power and control; the second no longer accepts this type of centralized control and wants to break paradigms. Some new players in the market have to be able to win in some way to survive.

This is the paradigm that the internet and the intelligent and disruptive applications have brought us. The digital revolution has given us free access to information, the dissemination of products and services. It broke the previous, comfortable model, which was in the hands of those who had the power.

Does cryptocurrency / crypto assets have the possibility of establishing itself as an alternative to physical currency?

Traditional banks already offer digital and remote services. However, opinions differ. Within the banking institutions, cryptocurrencies / crypto assets will be just a small step. Within the financial system, some people have difficulty understanding what "cyberspace" is. They are not used to digital tools, so they are more resistant to new technologies. On the other hand, some support and are very open to these new trends but who, unfortunately, have no internal support. They are blocked in their attempts at evolution and change.

The design of mechanisms / incentives, one of the most beautiful areas of applied microeconomics, is now being oriented in the design of crypto-economic applications, the well-known Apps.

Economic modeling, if well designed, can correctly anticipate problems not yet revealed by the data. A well-known case in macroeconomics is the relationship between inflation and unemployment, the so-called Phillips Curve, which Milton Friedman criticized and readjusted, indicating that the policies previously made were inflationary. This was not easy to capture in data; however, later, Friedman's thesis proved correct.

The use of functional economic theory in crypto assets is fundamental, mainly because the data is still reluctant to share facts or, worse, the circumstances change too quickly. For example, what explains the daily unpredictability in the use of Bitcoin? There are times when transactions are more or less variable, which seems to relate to the level of prices, attention given to the currency, and some seasonality.

There are econometric problems in integrating such data. Even the modeling of this unpredictability presents challenges: there is instability in the parameters. In other words, there is not a single model that explains the whole trajectory of the data since 2010.

Finally, we also have those who are entirely familiar with the new paradigms. However, they still prefer a fully sovereign currency, from a fiduciary state. The traditional bank has rejected this model for the same reasons that it has rejected other models for such a long time. This has led to the emergence of new Digital Banks in cyberspace, which would make available what the traditional bank does not offer. That is why it is impossible to stop the cryptocurrency or crypto assets system.

It is worth mentioning that although there are still reservations, as we have already mentioned above, several cases of countries and central banks are already using Blockchain for various purposes and some for their future Blockchain Encrypted Digital Currencies, with permitted structures and some with decentralized structures but with restricted writing.

As long as there is the internet, they will be embedded in their DNA, and it is irreversible. They will never disappear. The great need now is regulation. Using cryptocurrencies solves the problem of currency exchange boundaries. We now have a currency that is valid in any country, regardless of its sovereignty.

CRYPTOCURRENCY / CRYPTO ASSETS AND THE MARKET

What defines the value of the cryptocurrency / crypto assets is the law of demand and supply (in real-time). The blockchain and cryptocurrencies system does not allow issuing currency for an indefinite time. There is no objective way to exceed the maximum limit of money around the world. Any cryptocurrency that is created has a maximum supply of existence, which cannot be exceeded.

For Bitcoin, the maximum supply is 21 million. It is worth mentioning that cryptocurrencies are divisible. Bitcoin is divisible up to 8 decimals, which in Bitcoin terms, it is given the name of Satoshi, in honor of the creator of the cryptocurrency.

Is there a risk of cryptocurrencies losing their value due to too many available units?

When speaking in terms of risk, there are cryptocurrency / crypto assets exchanges around the world. They are universally valid "Digital Stock Exchanges," working uninterruptedly. Despite all the security, the investor may take risks, just as in any other investment in shares, when held in these exchanges.

It is a volatile economy due to:

1.   Low acceptance by most countries and there is not enough volume yet;

2.   Lack of regulation from governments responsible for the prevention of illicit activities;

3.   A limited number of Stock Exchanges, with many unregulated;

4.   Platforms - many informal and anonymous comparative websites without any legal certainty and transparency like the leader www.coinmarketcap.com, which has already been reported a few times by the community of traders and holders for errors and manipulation of information in the digital asset market in its platform and was recently bought by Binance – One of the largest exchange in the world, which in my understanding, may

bring uneasiness, suspicion, and conflict of interest with other trades in the market, due to Binance's leadership as a global exchange, now controlling coinmarketcap.com, which is fed with the information of the other exchange by API.

5.   In addition to the leading website, we recommend other comparative websites, such as:

https://www.cryptocurrencychart.com,

https://cointracking.info

https://www.quandl.com

https://www.cryptocompare.com

https://walletinvestor.com

https://nomics.com

https://www.coinhills.com

https://www.coingecko.com

6.   Recognition of States, Regulators, and Central Banks that this movement is at the core of a new generation that does not accept manipulation and having their finances manipulated by financial institutions that dictate rules and leverage their operations with the resources of their clients, shareholders and investors, and in the end, they dictate the rules of what you can and cannot with your own

money, and how much, when and how you can dispose of it, also without offering any guarantee other than fiduciary insurance, which covers only a certain amount. However, some cryptocurrencies / crypto assets do not provide any backing for value.

New Blockchain-based technologies that are changing careers, professions, the job market, and digital entrepreneurship:

GovTech

LegalTech

HeathTech

CovidTech

InsurTech

CryptoTech

FinTech

MobileTech

StockMktTech

RealStateTech

SmartCityTech, and others.

Platform Blockchain Venture Capital: Digital https://dlbx.io

Investment Fund of Crypto Assets: https://www.hashdex.com.br/

Chapter 7

How to become a Professional Crypto Trader (Obtaining Extraordinary Profits)

Crypto Trader of Cryptocurrency / Crypto Assets: Always study Technical Analysis and Graphic Patterns, and become familiar with the signals.

This is practically an extra chapter of learning about Crypto Trade and is hugely misunderstood by the vast majority of enthusiasts and holders in the cryptocurrency community. Failure in observing it is because many believe that the indicators are "market prophecies." It is fundamental that you know how to identify high and low patterns, and also how speculative bubble patterns work.

The chart below is a Wall Street bubble pattern and is also for the cryptocurrency market, as graphic patterns do not measure assets, they measure human behavior.

We are saying that these tools are definitely not divination tools or market prophecy, and should not be taken literally, as many ends up adopting these tools work like a compass only to point out trends.

Who decides where to go or which path to take is you, when you are operating directly, or the artificial intelligence of Robots when adopted.

In the image below, we give Ethereum as an example, analyzing a scale since its launch in Poliniex, its first sharp decrease (called the Bubble). Still, when compared to the relational pattern, it is relatively close to the stabilization of its price to start a new growth cycle.

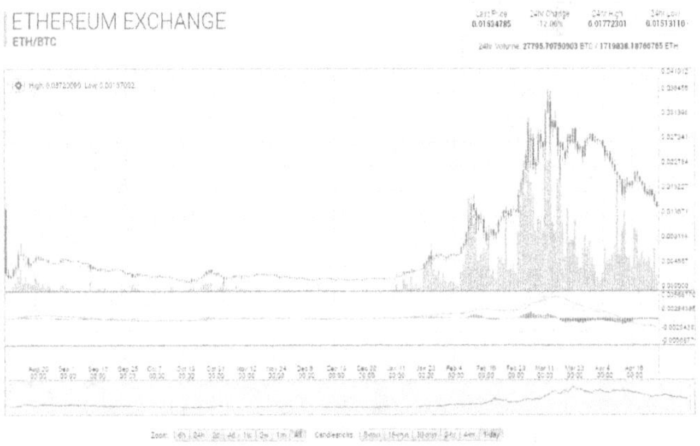

On the Trading View website, there are several updated chart analyses by more experienced users, which can help you to better understand the signals, behaviors, and the functioning of this Crypto Trader market.

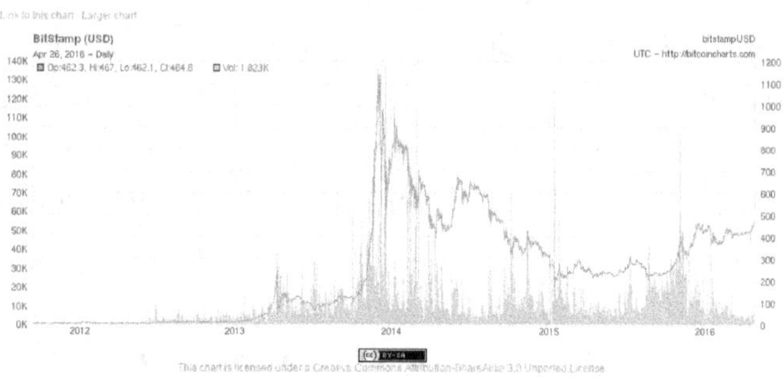

Attention to identify the whales

In the Crypto Trade language, the market is the sea, small investors are always called sardines, and the exponents are whales, which is, large cryptocurrency concentrators that, even if momentarily, can influence the volume and price of crypto assets in the market.

With this market extremely volatile, the sea of altcoins and tokens is the perfect habitat for the practice of Pump and Dump, something like inflating and dumping.

With a considerable volume of bitcoins and another cryptocurrency / crypto assets and tokens, mainly in some markets (exchange) with low volume, the whale enters and buys a good part of the open orders, raising the price exponentially, but artificially, without being organic to sustain capacity and price.

Sometimes attracted by the fat percentage, sardines rush toward the artificial potential of that currency or crypto asset and buy high priced orders created superficially or artificially by Whale Robot (they usually use bots to do this). When they reach the desired return, the whale dumps all the coins bough, throwing the price down again, causing considerable damage to the sardines, which in theory would be the beginner and inexperienced Crypto Trader.

It is also necessary to understand that there is a real possibility of making a profit by following the trends and movements of the whales. Still, we need to be an astute sardine, because in general, a whale swallows a sardine, and a sardine will never swallow a whale.

In this market, you can dare, but when you have more experience and a history of success, at that moment, prudence and caution are essential.

Finally, understand that you should never concentrate all your eggs in one basket.

If you are thinking of starting in the Crypto Trade market, I recommend that you start with your own capital, and be aware and willing to lose at the first moment, so it establishes a risk ceiling, that you can learn by gaining more and also by losing. In this world of Crypto Trader, it is essential to start with limited resources and be willing to lose a large part, so then you can move forward with more consistency.

With the exception of Bitcoin – BTC, ETH, LTC, do no concentrate more than 10% of your capital on other crypto assets that have been on the market for more than 12 months, yet, analyze where these crypto assets are listed, the size of their market, the quantity of supply and the history presented, for example in coinmarketcap.com and other comparative websites, such as https://wallentinvestor.com/ which has less superficial analyzes.

The exception of the recommendation above would be when it comes to a new project, with a well-defined purpose, a well-founded White Paper, with a team with notorious knowledge and excellent reputation, projects with ballast and backing in physical assets would be the most recommendable.

These are just basic tips for those just starting; you will create your own tactics and strategies according to the knowledge and experience you will be acquiring over the months.

Technical Analysis context: why is this so necessary for a trader? It is simple! It is the technical analysis that allows us to understand what is actually happening on the chart, being used by all traders, from beginners to experts. But before you get into that technical issue, do you know why prices fluctuate? This is a persistent question of those who are starting in the market: why does the price change, and how does it occur?

First, we must understand that behind these graphs, there are thousands of people who do their readings and look for future projections of what an asset can do. These same people have different interests in the market and are subject to mixed emotions, such as fear, greed, frustration, and ecstasy.

One of the factors that make the market move is the LAW OF OFFER AND DEMAND, and we can explain it as forces that dictate the price of an asset and make its price vary. If there is an abundant supply of an asset, and few people looking for it, the cost of that asset tends to fall; likewise, if there is an asset with high demand, but with limited supply, its price tends to rise, due to its scarcity.

A straightforward example of this is Bitcoin, which has a limited offer. Satoshi Nakamoto, its creator, limited it to 21 million, that is, Bitcoin is not a currency that can be printed without limits and cannot be offered endlessly, as it is a revolutionary cryptocurrency, that brings countless benefits, its valuation increases year after year since the demand for Bitcoin has grown more and more, while its offer remains fixed and cannot be changed. This causes its price to be high, giving more value to this asset.

Another factor that influences the price fluctuation is that people behind the market do not always read the same graph of what is happening, and different analysis causes the price to move because someone did some wrong analysis and lost money to the market. That is why a correct study of the patterns that occur in the graph is critical. In this way, we can understand that there are forces behind the market, which are called bulls and bears, or either bullish versus bearish.

Bulls, or bullish, are identified when there is too much demand for an asset and too little supply, causing prices to rise. The name "bull" was chosen because when a bull attacks with its horns, it attacks from the bottom up, and in this case, raises the market prices. As for bears, bearish, they are identified when there is a lot of supply of an asset, however, few people are looking for it, causing a drop in its price. The term "bear" is given because of its attack that is with its paw from top to bottom, and in this case, overturns the market. When the market is on the rise, we say that there is a predominance of bulls, and when it is falling, we assume that bears are winning the fight.

Another essential strength in the market is the strength of whales. Whale is a term given to the big players in the market that operate with large capitals, aiming at high profits. Whales have the power to command the direction of the market, injecting a lot of money into assets that they believe will be highly valued. These players are cunning and enter specific points to make the most of what the market offers.

Unlike whales, there are also sardines, which are small groups of investors who enter with small capitals, seeking moderate profits and making a volume in the market. Unlike whales, sardines do not have the power to dictate the direction of the market, so knowledge is needed to understand the market forces and not go against them.

Once you understand the forces behind the graphs, you can now better understand the real concept of technical analysis.

Technical analysis, or graphical analysis as it is also known, is one of the most used techniques in the market, being the study of market action through the use of graphs that show the behavior of assets in the market, with the objective of identifying future movements of the assets, using techniques that lead us to understand the meaning of each variation in the graph. For example, we can project future Bitcoin movements based on studying its chart, looking at its behavior in the pat and using techniques such as support, resistance, trend analysis, Candlesticks, chart patterns, Fibonacci, and indicators. In summary, technical analysis is a set of methods and tools that seek to study the market's past and identify future projections for assets, enabling us to obtain gains day after day.

The graphical analysis serves both those who need to study an asset in a long-term, and those who want to profit from short-term volatility, because within the graphical analysis it is possible to select the graphical times you want to study, thus being able to observe the history of prices you want to analyze, and also chose the type of trader you want to use.

The existing trader types are scalper, day trader, swing trader, position, and hold. The difference between them is the graphical time that we use in our analysis. On a scalper, for example, we analyze in short graphs from 1 minute to 5 minutes. Some traders even trade in seconds on this classification. The day trader, on the other hand, is open and closed on the same day, using a chart ranging from 15 minutes to 1 hour.

The swing trader is a type of trader in which you can open a trade and take up to 7 days to complete it, observing more 4-hour and daily charts. The position is a trader that usually takes weeks to happen and aims at much larger targets, based on daily and weekly charts. And finally, we have the hold, which is a type of trader that takes months and even years and aims at huge future projections, using weekly and monthly charts as a basis.

And what all these classifications have in common: graphic analysis. All of them are based on techniques to understand the resourcefulness of prices and to get the maximum profit from the market with the lowest possible risk, and the first step for you to understand the graphic analysis is to understand what PRICE ACTION is.

Price action means the action performed by the price, that is, any movement of the price upwards or downwards, in any graph, of any market. The price action is the study of the "naked" chart, which is, without the addition of any other tool, such as indicators, studying only what the market is offering us.

This reading can happen in different types of charts: it can be in line charts, which only considers the closing price of the asset; on the Renko chart, which is timeless; bar graphs, which show the opening and closing of the asset according to the selected time; or through the best known and used by all traders, the candlestick chart, which will be addressed shortly.

All of these charts reflect the beliefs and actions of all participants who operate and trade in the market over a period of time, and these beliefs are depicted on the market price chart in the form of "price action," giving evidence of what may happen. Thus, support, resistance, and trends are essential to identify possible price reactions well.

But, what are supports and resistance?

Well, this is a fundamental issue for every trader. In all of our analyses, we must always seek support and resistance before anything else.

Realistically, imagine the floor of your house; it is the support of the entire structure that is above it. Likewise, graphics are zones, or price levels, where price support exists; this support can be understood as a powerful buying force. This means that the price tends to fall and hit these zones and, after that, to revert, forming funds, which are the minimum that the cost of that asset has reached. You can identify these zones as they are places that the price often touches and reverses, as shown in the chart below.

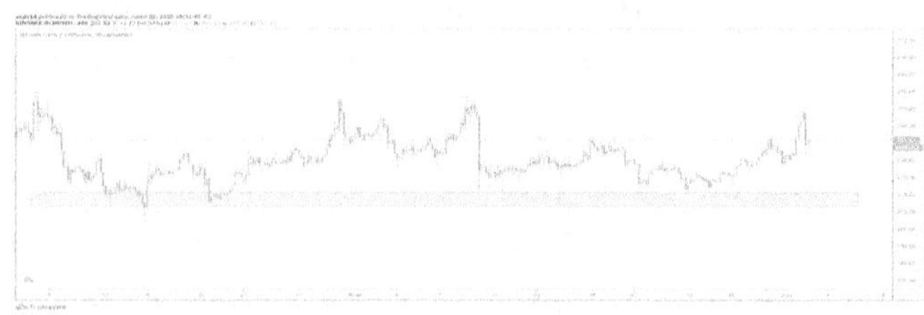

Figure 1: H4 chart of BCH / USDT showing a support zone.

With the resistances, it is almost the same thing, but in the opposite. In the case of resistances, we can compare with the ceiling of your house, where we say it is a construction limit. Thus, graphic resistances are price levels where there is more substantial selling pressure, and prices tend to hit those levels and fall again, forming tops through the maximums that the asset price reached, as shown in the graph below.

Figure 2: H4 graph of BCH / USDT showing a resistance zone at the top.

But, why in these zones the price tends to react inversely? It has to do with our emotions. Many operators identify support, and right there, they place their purchase, or see resistance and position their sales, trusting that there will be a reversal in the asset's movement. This is called the collective memory of investors and is something that every trader develops throughout his operations.

However, as we always say, supports and resistances are there to be broken! If it were not so, there would be no oscillations that would give us profit in the market. Therefore, you must pay attention to the supports and resistances that we must operate.

One thing that is very important and you should know well is that, after the break of support, that same support becomes a resistance, and after the break of resistance, that same resistance becomes support. It is possible to see in this example in the Bitcoin chart. The asset breaks the resistance, and that same resistance becomes support.

Figure 3: H4 graph of BTC / USDT showing a broken resistance zone.

After understanding what support and resistance are, we can mention one more issue that is essential for us traders to operate with excellence: the trend. Understanding the asset trend is extremely important for any trader. This is because the trend is the direction in which the asset moves, or the direction in which the market, in general, is moving.

By knowing how to identify a trend, the trader can find good points of purchase, being able to buy a cheap asset, which, consequently, increases his profits in operations. On a graph, the trend can be seen by analyzing tops (resistances) and bottoms (supports), as the market moves in a zigzag pattern, building patterns that allow us to draw lines and identify crucial points of the asset.

These are four types of trend: the first is the upward trend. In this trend, prices reach higher tops than the previous ones, and also higher bottoms, that is, we have rising tops and bottoms. Joining these bottoms, we can draw a line called UTL, or upward trend line.

Figure 4: Representation of a UTL on the BNB / BTC chart

The second type of trend is a downward trend. In this trend, we always find tops that are lower than those previously formed, and also, the bottoms are always smaller than the previous ones; that is, the tops and bottoms are increasingly cheaper, being, therefore, descendants. By joining these tops, we can draw a DTL, or downward trend line, thus identifying that there is a downward trend here.

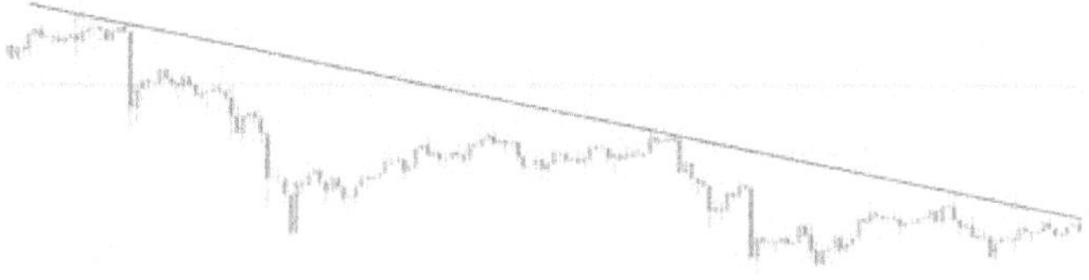

Figure 5: Representation of a DTL on the BCT / USDT chart

You must understand that we must always follow the trend in our operations; therefore, the importance of correctly identifying the current trend of the asset that will operate. This reduces the risk of your operations, increasing the likelihood of high gains in your results.

UTL's and DTL's are also considered as supports and resistances. This is because it is common for prices to reach these levels and continue with their trends.

There is also the lateral tendency, also known as the congestion zone. There are times when the market simply lateralizes, forming a lateral trend characterized by tops and bottoms at the same price level. In this type of trend, when we join the bottoms, we have support, and when we enter the tops, we have a resistance.

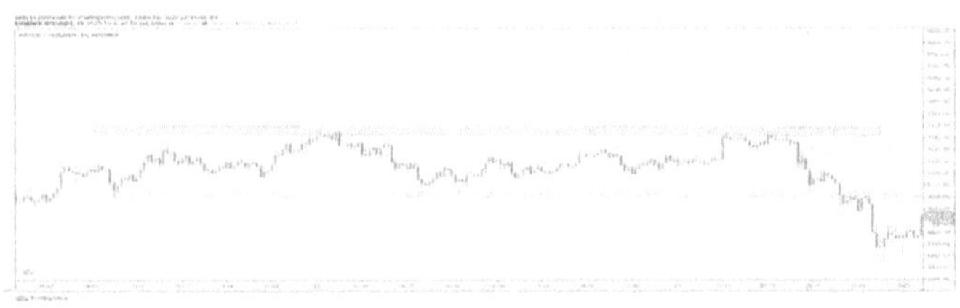

Figure 6: Representation of a lateral trend on the BTC / USDT chart

The fourth and final trend is a trend that is not always considered by many, but we cannot stop talking about it: it is the undefined trend. Why undefined? Its name says it all; in this trend, we are unable to identify tops and bottoms that can be joined, thus finding an uncertainty in the asset. Operating on a trend like this requires care, as we are not sure where the asset is moving to.

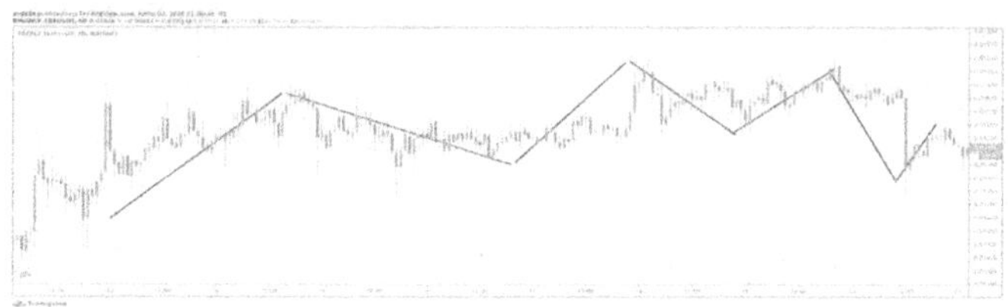

Figure 7: Representation of an undefined trend on the TRX / USDT chart

A pattern of continuity characterizes every trend. If the trend is upward, the tops and bottoms are ascending, if it is downward, the tops and bottoms are descending, if it is lateral, the tops and bottoms are at the same price level, and so on.

However, when there is a break in this pattern, we say that there is a reversal in the trend because, as was mentioned above, supports and resistances are also broken. For example, let's say we have an upward trend, but at a certain point, the tops are no longer higher than the previous ones. The market may then start to reverse its trend.

For a trend to reverse, the trend line must be broken. When this happens, we say that the asset has broken the trend line, and from there, we can start a safer trader. If an asset breaks its UTL, there is a possibility that we will be sold, if it breaks a DTL, there is a possibility that we will be bought into the asset. If the market is sideways, it can break support and set up a sale or break resistance and set up a buy. In the case of undefined trends, there must be tops and bottoms that are clear and can be identified.

When a trend line is broken, it is common to occur in a formation called pivot. Pivot is the first inversion of a standard sequence in the trend; it is a kind of "breath" that the asset gives to continue its reversal. Through the pivot, we have a more explicit confirmation that the trend has been reversed, and we can carry out our trader.

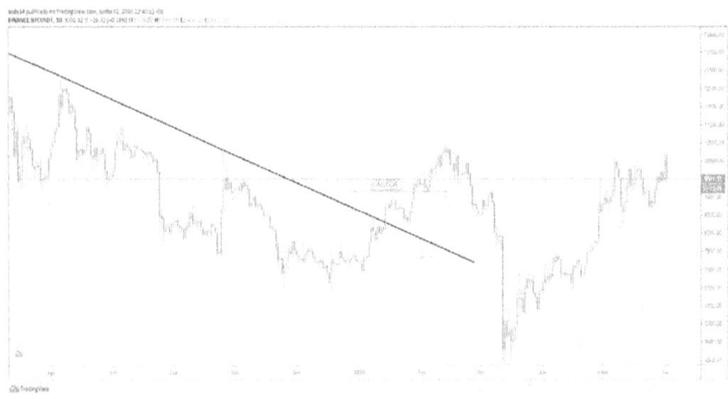

Figure 8: Representation of a pivot

After breaking a trend line, the ideal entry would be precisely at the break of the pivot head, so we would be sure that the trend was reversed. That is, if you are a trader who does not like to wait too much, you can start trading when the trend breaks, but if you are a safer trader and want to wait for confirmation, just wait for a pivot and start trading after it.

There is also an essential graph tool that helps you to identify possible reversals of trends. These tools are candlesticks, or to put it simply, candles. These are patterns represented by vertical bars of different shapes and sizes and are rich in information about asset trading.

In a candle, we can know the opening price of the trade at the selected chart time, the closing price of the trade, and also the maximum and the minimum variations that occurred during that time. These variations are demonstrated in the form of shadows or wicks. There are top candles and bottom candles, and within these patterns, there are candles that inform us of possible reversals in the asset.

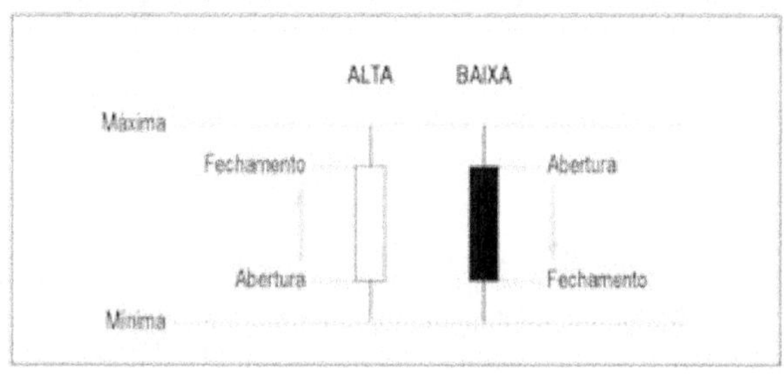

Figure 9: Representation of the formation of a candle.

Among the reversal candles, we can mention the Doji. This is a type of candle in which its closing is at the opening or near it. In this case, we have indecision in the market.

Finding a candle like this in resistances or supports is an excellent sign that there is a possibility of asset reversal.

Figure 10: Representation of a Doji.

Another candle pattern that may indicate a reversal and you need to be aware of is the hammer, which can also be found on tops and bottoms. In this candle, we have the closing near the opening, with a lower shadow bellow it, and almost or sometimes no shadow at all above the candle.

Figure 11: Representation of a hammer.

A pattern very similar to the hammer is the falling star, which can also indicate a reversal, so we have to be aware. In this case, we have a huge shadow at the top of the candle, and little or no shadow at the bottom. This candle is also known as an inverted hammer.

Figure 12: Representation of a falling star.

A first alert, when starting your day of Crypto Trade, if you see everything red on the screen: Never panic. If you see everything green: Don't get carried away.

Chapter 8

Blockchain in the fight against corruption and crime

The Blockchain network, despite being idealized for its original foundation in the exchange of digital assets in the scope of finance and the new digital economy, presents opportunities and applications that can and certainly will be used in the fight against corruption and crime, starting this experience, especially in Brazil, within the scope of the GovTech 4.0 Program proposed by the National Institute of Excellence in Public Policies – INEPP, a Civil Society Organization of Public Interest – OSCIP, which I had the honor to be the founder, and again, assuming in 2020 as its current president.

a) The new Crypto Digital Economy dispenses with its exchange and settlement by intermediaries with no confidence – Two parties are able to make an exchange without the supervision or intermediation of a third party, significantly reducing or even eliminating the risk of the counterparty; Blockchain Technology, through a Smart Contract, functions as a Peer to Peer custodian and equally decentralized.

– User empowerment – Users are in control of all their information and transactions and do not depend on third parties and decide what to do and how to do with their data / information / digital assets;

– Reliable, decentralized and / or distributed data – Blockchain data is complete, consistent, traceable and recorded correctly in an unalterable, accurate and widely available ledger;

– Reliable and addictive lifetime data – Because networks are decentralized, the Blockchain network has no central point of failure and is more resistant to malicious attacks;

– Integrity and publicity – Users can trust that their transactions will be executed precisely as the protocol / algorithm determines, eliminating the need for a third party;

– Digital – any and all documents, data, assets, or services can be expressed in code form and encapsulated or referenced by an electronic ledger entry, which means that Blockchain technology still has much broader applications than those widespread, most of them have not yet been developed and much less implemented.

In the last decades, the concern about corruption has intensified all over the world, particularly in Brazil, changing even the system of government and ideological tendency prevalent for decades in the country, with legacy systems created by the bureaucracy to sell difficulties and buy ease, the basic principles for promoting corruption and impunity.

Corruption is one of the worst evils in society. It is cancer, which, if not combated with the right dosage, can take a large part of society to the ICU and then the bankruptcy of all its social, cultural, academic institutes, economic and social, with its ethical, moral and Christian transgressions.

On the other hand, we can imagine the countless possibilities that will be made available with the use of crypto assets or private digital cryptocurrencies for, in particular, when exchanged for possible legal Crypto Assets in Blockchain – State Crypto, for example:

– Realize, register, and control transfers of federal, state, and municipal funds, and track payments made by governments in all powers, levels, and spheres, through secure, authorized, but identified (named) Digital Crypt Wallets. This would be the first time that public money represented by its state-owned crypto asset would have a historical and immutable record, every time the crypto asset changed hands.

– Transfer funds to NGOs and other third sector organizations and control all payments and applications for particular purposes, which are also registered, permissioned, and nominated.

– Identify possible criminals through the use of duly licensed State or Private Crypto Assets, and eventually criminalize the commercialization of fake private crypto assets (without using blockchain and without making Blockchain Explorer publicly available), especially inhibiting the marketing of those Crypto Assets not listed in licensed brokers, or as the Central Bank is currently doing, include these digital crypto asset wallets in the PIX system, ensuring liquidity for licensed and integrated brokers.

– It is possible with this Open Crypto Bank model to mark suspicious digital wallets, and relating it to other duly licensed receivers and transferors of digital assets, we can be disruptive, develop a decentralized economy, even in the case of state crypto, with permissioned writing but public reading, generating transparency, security, and immutability of data and records. But we do not need and do not recommend that the purpose of Blockchain be distorted for anarchic purposes or aimed at protecting crimes typified in countries' criminal codes.

– Another relevant aspect would be the Federal Revenue through the integration with the Central Bank to be able to tax in licensed brokers and Blockchains of licensed digital assets, the Digital Tax at source, (inline equivalent to the old Brazilian CPMF, however, of a 100% digital activity which today does not contribute anything to the state or to society) so it will not burden people or companies. However, this digital tax should be applied in large part to invest in more applications capable of fighting corruption and organized crime as a whole and to sustain public health and safety services.

– Licensed Brokers should be obliged to create and adopt their own Tokens – Stable digital assets, and back them up with real physical assets of their owners or company, to avoid scams, fraud or improper investment capture, including promoting self-rafting in their databases, to justify their paralysis or judicial intervention.

– Establish a unification, standardization, and adoption of a decentralized database in Blockchain within the scope of the Ministry of

Justice, Public Security, Central Bank, Federal Revenue, Federal Police, Public Ministry, Judiciary, Legislative and other entities, using the Blockchain GovTech 4.0, and making it public, auditable and accessible to all instances of the Federal Executive, Federal Legislative and Federal Judiciary, extending it to States and Municipalities.

– Apply the content of the LGPD (General Data Protection Law) recently approved by the Brazilian national congress, within the scope of the Blockchain GovTech 4.0, and compel the implementation of its resources within the range of private crypto assets and licensed brokers in Brazil, considering the characteristic of Cryptography that is already peculiar and mandatory in Blockchain.

The value registered in the Blockchain is not just a number to be published, but it is the financial transfer itself, which defines the existence of the currency. In this way, fraud is practically impossible, if the architecture is decentralized, even if allowed but with its public blockchain explorer.

Brazilian public institutions in the recent past have been less than efficient in monitoring and controlling the use of public funds and tax waivers. Also, Brazil spends a lot of time and public resources in the fight against corruption, without a joint and articulated action between the different organs of the State, at all levels, spheres, and powers.

Besides, the country still uses legacy systems that are outdated, insecure, and easy to manipulate, which makes integration, transparency, and tracking of data - information difficult. Therefore, the use of Blockchain would be a fast, efficient, secure, transparent solution and with complete interoperability with other blockchain and licensed brokers.

Brazil also wastes many public resources with NGOs and other third sector organizations due to the lack of decentralized and transparent technology, and in this case, specifically, it could even constitute a Blockchain model that is equally allowed but distributed, since data mining (cyber data mining) in niche projects, for economic, social, educational, cultural, environmental and other purposes, can generate and distribute tokens that encourage or even require the involvement and participation of organized civil society in monitoring and control on the application of public resources in projects of public interest, with financial compensation for these digital assets.

The world will need to learn to live with disruptive, decentralized, distributed models and increasingly assimilate the new and disruptive mode of digital transactions Peer to Peer, especially in the field of finance and the 100% digital economy, with cryptocurrencies or crypto assets be of an open and distributed private nature, but with a public, transparent and auditable display and reading on a blockchain explorer, or of a public, decentralized but permitted nature and also with a public, transparent and verifiable reading on the blockchain explorer, where it is essential to demonstrate public interest in this new digital economy, while still generating and distributing financial and social results according to the type and purpose of each project / initiative.

There will still be absolutely anonymous, untraceable blockchain systems and transactions in decentralized systems, or between distributed blockchains, however, whether today in the form of Fiduciary Money, or tomorrow in the way of State Cryptocurrency, the state will never stop being sovereign over its forced currency, although no longer fiduciary, now as a legal course in Blockchain, where the ballast with real assets will be necessary, such as gold for example, and other tangible assets.

I understand that if the Central Bank comes to assume the settlement platform of the Private Crypto Asset Market duly listed and approved in Open, Closed or Permitted Blockchain, as the Central Bank of Brazil is doing at the moment, with the new Instant Payment system - PIX as an example, and also encourage, the Open Crypto Bank, (Digital Banks with a license to operate in Blockchain with Crypto State Regulated and Self-Regulated Private Assets) forcing them to open the APIs.

As the Open Bank of the Regulated Banking sector is already in process, the tendency is to reduce the demand for this alternative, anonymous and technologically prepared platforms to ensure the anonymity and confidentiality of their holders, and which, in fact, are and will remain for a long time, outside the system regulated by its technology and algorithmic architecture.

Now, if Governments understand that the taxation of a digital tax should be minimal, simplified, and convenient to generate the transaction hash track, and, of course, contribute to increasing its collection, in a multi-billion sector, which does not contribute at all to the state nor for society, withholding tax, without bi-contribution or bi-taxation, this in itself will discourage the good citizen, in the adoption of these super mentioned crypto assets, and inhibit the use of these alternative and anonymous platforms, that can bring civil and criminal liability with the consequent penal application.

It is already a consensus in the community that what they truly seek and desire is to exercise their freedom to choose which economy they wish to be in, in the highly regulated state digital economy, to protect the national and international financial system, or in the private and digital economy self-regulated, whether from companies and specialized platforms (Fintechs or CryptoTechs) or from private banks.

However, it is important that private Digital Platforms (financial – FinTech or Crypto Assets – CryptoTech) from PIX, remain independent from the hold of banks authorized and regulated by the Central Bank, for primary and low-risk services and simplified compliance, offering solutions and a better experience for users who do not want and are not required to become account holders of traditional banks, and even they are not interested in this low-income and more informal market.

I understand that for Governments or Central Banks, the less Government / State and the more Private Initiative and People are in control of their money or digital assets, (State or Private) the less need for regulation, inspection and combating evasion, and more freedom and self-regulation, provided that at the end, we have a kind of a Crypto PIX with interoperability between blockchain registered in Central Banks, to settle transactions in State Crypto or also in other Private Crypto duly Licensed in Blockchain platforms of Central Banks integrated by API throughout the world.

We cannot ignore that BIT Coin – BTC, its various Forks (Bifurcations) and some altcoins already established in an absolutely distributed way, which are among the top 30 in the Coin Market Capital ranking, will remain as an alternative and parallel system to the regulated state model, following the original line of disruption of the traditional financial and monetary sector, for the self-regulating private cryptocurrency system, which I am mentioning in this chapter, however, the settlement on Permitted or Licensed Platforms registered with Central Banks.

As it is recognized the State Licensed Digital Currencies and Equally Licensed Private Assets, listed exclusively in equally licensed and regulated brokers, this will result in attracting a good part of this new Coin Market Cap, to a new system / platform of settlement and monetization, regulated or self-regulating.

However, a new class of state revenue is created, which would be the contributor of the

Digital Tax that can generate more autonomy and wealth for the state and its partners in the sector of Public and Private Crypto Assets, by distributing this same wealth to society and not just as it does in the current system, generating the distribution of profits and dividends restricted to shareholders of the traditional banking and financial system, who will continue, but returning to their original and fundamental role of raising and lending fiduciary and / or Digital – Virtual money.

Cryptocurrencies or Crypto Assets with a decentralized and distributed nature will always exist in this new disruptive digital economy, and the Peer to Peer market is an irreversible reality, understanding that its products will still be in a decentralized and potentially distributed manner; however, it has already been recognized by the Central Bank of Brazil that, production of data mining of crypto assets is considered for the purposes of the digital economy as production so that it can be counted in the country's trade balance and incorporated into the Central Bank's reserves.

In particular, the motivation was naturally for BitCoin – The most prevalent Crypto Asset in the market. However, it should apply to any other crypto asset listed in brokers that are licensed and approved by the Central Bank of Brazil and by API in other Central Banks throughout the International Open Crypto Bank.

Chapter 9

Blockchain in environmental preservation and recovery

Blockchain in environmental preservation, measurement, accounting, and socio-environmental compensation, with tokenization of digital assets and monetization on permissioned, decentralized, but controlled platforms.

The global concern with environmental preservation has been responsible for a real change in the mentality of nations, which currently seek sustainable development instead of expanding the economy at any price and under any circumstances.

In this sense, an essential tool found by several countries to protect the environment and, simultaneously, generate revenue, for their own preservation and recovery, was environmental taxation, and of course, even better if digital through a native Crypto Asset, in this case, I'm referring to the Amazonas Coin Project that I was a consultant, and with my team, we provided all the technology for a Blockchain with consensus proof and 100% Native Multi Wallet, and Data Mining and management of Green CrowdFunding through OSCIP - INEPP which also I was honored to be its founder.

Simply, this form of taxation has two aspects:

• Extra Fiscal – consistent with the increase in charges on potentially polluting activities, to discourage them;

• Tax-related to the collection of fees that cover the State's environmental inspection activity.

In both cases, we could establish a utility TOKEN and TOKEN security through a smart contract, to issue digital environmental money, to control and monetize on licensed exchanges / platforms.

In this context, it is clear that the world pioneers in the implementation of environmental tax laws are the countries of the European continent. In Germany, Sweden, Holland, France, United Kingdom, and Denmark there are already several tax species that aim at environmental protection, however, when we analyze them, they are not the best examples of ecological preservation and recovery, since they occupy in their respective territories, high concentrations of land used for their Agro

Business activities, impacting the climate and the environment.

In this reality, the increase in rates on highly polluting vehicles, the incidence of taxes on vegetation removal, the creation of taxes on CO_2 emissions, among others, can be cited as examples. In the Brazilian reality, however, there are still timid steps towards the regulation of taxes with these characteristics.

It is worth noting, with this global scenario, that the positive environmental impacts of this archaic tax system are minimal when compared to international experience. In this way, there is an urgent need for reform, reorganizing state revenue to ensure a better balance between economic and environmental development.

It is salutary to remember, however, that the creation of new tax species may represent, among other economic and social problems, an increase in State spending on the collection and inspection of payments, as well as the worsening of the – already gigantic – bureaucracy of the obligations imposed on taxpayers when paying taxes.

An innovative solution to this complication may be in blockchain technology, which was initially developed to solve problems related to transactions with crypto assets or cryptocurrencies, avoiding duplication and recording all operations on the ledger, which in simplified language, can be understood as a fully licensed virtual and for life, book of records.

In the blockchain, financial transactions are more efficient, due to the elimination of intermediaries and the instantaneous transfer, without, however, losing security, since the data is identified and encrypted. In this sense, we can be close to a solution for each country, which would be the Tokenization of Environmental Preservation and Conservation activities.

In this case, regardless of environmental taxation issues, native and national crypto assets, respecting the sovereignty and independence of each nation, could establish their own quantifications and qualifications to assign value to each crypto asset, which using the blockchain, can demonstrate with absolute transparency and traceability the use of digital resources and the appropriate compensation and monetization due to the real application in the projects of protection, preservation and environmental and climate recovery.

The innovations brought by blockchain are not restricted to that. The technology already allows the elaboration of smart-contracts, which consist of lines of code that register, above all, agreements of wills, executing them in an autonomous way. For example, in a purchase and sale smart contract, payment can be instantaneous, and calculated in the same way in the event of a payment delay, with interest and monetary correction, as well as automatic registration and without the intermediation of the new ownership of an asset, product or service.

In this context we participated in an extraordinary project called Amazonas Coin – www.amazonascoin.com.br which is a crypto asset 100% developed by Brazilians, being a speculative model, with Open Blockchain, based on the PoC – Proof of Capacity consensus, with the most ecological data mining system (cyber mining) considered the most ecological and correctly environmental mining technology of the entire Blockchain ecosystem, which allows for greater decentralization with minimal cost of natural resources, since it uses approximately 1/500 fraction of the energy consumed by other consensus evidence.

On the other hand, we created the Voluntary Environmental Compensation Token, called Amazonas Token – AMT, with blockchain, consensus proof and native multi Wallet called PoP – Proof of Participation, using Cloud Data Mining, where there are practically no mining or transaction costs for assets using the Blockchain PoP.

SUBCHAPTER 9.1

Carbon Credit Tokenization – AMZT

The situation

Recently, fires in the Amazon have drawn the attention of the entire world to the region. The countries claim that Brazil is not respecting international conventions and collaborating to increase the temperature on Earth, contrary to what was agreed in Paris at the UN world environmental forum.

However, Brazil is not among the six biggest polluters on the planet, which are: China, the United States, India, Russia, and Japan, followed by the sum of the countries of the European Union.

Amazon is composed of riverside and indigenous Brazilians who suffer from the same problem; lack of necessary infrastructure and the need to scale up their economic activities. In the meantime, we have a situation of logistical flow from the interior to the more developed cities like Manaus and Belém.

The main arteries of the Amazon are the Amazon and Negro rivers. The cities located upstream towards the borders between Brazil,

Venezuela, Colombia, and Peru have a terrible flow of organic and inorganic waste and an insufficient production to strengthen the logistical supply flow.

There is also a tendency for the government to encourage the exploration of economic activities in the soil and subsoil of indigenous reserves, as well as the promotion of inputs to those that can generate wealth through fishing and high-yield agricultural production; An unexplored land with a real need for development.

Carbon credits can be traded in exchange for preserving forests in private riverside areas and in private areas of recurrent extraction, such as plantations of chestnut, syringe, etc., which do not need to be cut to generate wealth.

Millions and millions of kilometers are perfectly preserved in the Amazon and these people who preserve it, receive nothing for maintaining the land this way; just an example of this untapped potential that occurs in several municipalities in the Amazon region.

So there is a dilemma; how to generate wealth in the Amazon region without harming the environment? How can the digital economy enhance this?

What is the carbon credit

The reduction in greenhouse gas emissions can be measured by a metric unit: carbon credit. A carbon credit is the representation of a ton of carbon that is no longer emitted into the atmosphere, contributing to the reduction of the greenhouse effect and to a decrease of the Earth's temperature by 2 degrees Celsius in 30 years, according to the UN goals.

This benefit can be issued by improving energy efficiency, such as the replacement of fossil fuels in electrical, manufacturing, and other plants with sustainable fuels such as hydroelectric, solar, biomass, or wind. It can also be obtained by reducing deforestation or naturally preserving forests that could, by law, be replaced by profitable economic activities.

Thus, based on the difference in gas emissions between each energy matrix or voluntary maintenance of the standing forest, units of carbon credits can be issued and can be traded on the financial market.

This way, it can be seen that carbon credit may become the wealth-generating factor for isolated or degraded communities, guaranteeing them a sustainable standard of living with horizons of improvement and cognitive, educational, social, and economic growth.

How carbon is sequestered (removed) from the air

The Amazon rainforest is home to about 20% of all the fauna and flora on the planet. There are more than 30 thousand species of animals, some not yet cataloged, which are estimated to comprise a population of more than 30 million. There are more than 15,000 species of plants, with more than 300 listed annually, according to WWF.

This rich diversity presents combinations of species that, together with the others, sequester carbon from the atmosphere, more than they release. One example is the system of Seringa and Castanheira-do-Brasil. This biological consortium allows a rational exploration of both cultures and efficient carbon sequestration, allowing a sensible exploration of their potential for development, production, longevity, and viability of its system economic value.

A Seringa tree (rubber tree) can withdraw 135 carbon credits in 30 years, being a productive activity, this means that the preserved forest around the extraction area of the syringe, as well as the castanha-do-Brasil (chestnut) exploration, contains an asset above USD$ 50 billion in carbon credits over a 30-year horizon.

How carbon is traded in Brazil

REED+ in Brazil – Law 12.727 of 2012, of Environmental Legislation, encourages the conservation of the environment, as well as the adoption of technologies and good practices that reconcile forest productivity, with reduction of environmental impacts, as a way of promoting development ecologically sustainable.

Among the points of this law is the payment or incentive to environmental services such as remuneration, monetary or not, for the activities of conservation and improvement of ecosystems and that generate environmental services, such as how to put the sequestration, preservation, maintenance and increase inventory, and the decrease in carbon flow.

This legal support for environmental services helps to structure the carbon market in the country, which is not regulated. Brazil aims to reduce deforestation in the Amazon rainforest, invest in measures that help mitigate GHG emissions, and must establish a mechanism for environmental valuation.

In 2017, Law 13,576 / 2017 was created, which deals with the national Biofuels policy (RENOVABIO), whose objective is to expand production based on environmental, economic, and social sustainability compatible with the growth of this market.

The RENOVABIO Law creates an obligation to offset carbon credits for fuel distributors. The creation of this obligation created a market still unexplored in Brazil and with many opportunities in the digital world.

The Brazilian market received funds from the sale of carbon credits by the BNDES with deposits in the Amazon Fund, since 2007. In 13 years, Norway distributed more than USD$ 1 billion and Germany more than USD$ 0.025 billion. However, as of 2019, due to inadequacies in the compliance process, and lack of information about the preservation of forests in Brazil, the Amazon Fund has been "dehydrated" and is losing importance day by day.

This dehydration and the promotion of trade in voluntary carbon credit, that is, environmental compensation made autonomously by companies / organizations that have sustainable programs in their structures, have been heating the market. Several companies are protecting areas and commercializing these compensations, adding value to the products of the sponsoring companies.

In this context, the tokenization of carbon credits issued by a certified or non-certified project is taking shape. The creation of securitized tokens, based on environmental preservation, generating value, and returning as wealth to needy communities that do not have access to job creation processes, previously dependent on government humanitarian aid programs, become now an exciting future vision.

Social Environmental Compensations (Amazonas Token - AMT)

Crypto crowdfunding is a way of raising funds for causes, businesses, and people. The funds raised in this modality can be used for the controlled and sustainable socio-environmental development of any communities or areas, with the security of traceability in the use of such resources, which gives transparency and credibility to the resulting actions.

Is it possible to raise funds to develop degraded and isolated areas through a reliable and transparent, flexible, scalable crypto crowdfunding and have a massive transformational purpose aligned with the goals of the millennium and that is capable of being associated with the maximum of people and companies, creating a crowd of followers?

Yes, it is possible. Just tokenize the voluntary environmental compensation, transforming it into certified encrypted Digital Tokens, to be used in social projects, generating wealth and financing local impact projects, managed by local authorities, without government intermediation and in a traceable way, via blockchain. This is the proposal of ecosystems like the Amazonascoin.

The Amazon Token Business Model

The basic premise for the operation of the Amazonas Token is its collateralization with the value of the global socio-environmental compensation, which can be a secure representation, a security token, to be issued to each voluntary or imposing environmental asset in custody.

As a reference only, the value of carbon credit in 2020 is close to USD$ 23.00, however, the World Bank estimates that by 2030 this value will be close to USD$ 80.00.

The Blockchain Platform Amazon Token safeguards the equivalent of 19 million Environmental Assets (Digital Token) for voluntary or imposing environmental compensation, in partnership with a hotel located in the interior of the legal Amazon.

The idea is that these Environmental Digital Assets benefit the communities adjacent to the hotel, transforming the local society and economy that suffer even from the absence of electricity, in the middle of the 21st century.

In areas degraded by years of rubber exploitation, replanting of rubber trees and chestnut trees can be carried out to explore the benefits of carbon sequestration, instead of exploring natural rubber or the processing of chestnuts, which could be other sustainable activities, but would be explored in a secondary and complementary way.

The trees planted in the chestnut – seringa system are capable of hijacking 135 carbon credits, each in 30 years, which enables them to be certified and receive resources via crypto crowdfunding in exchange for custody of the generated credit certificates; The digital economy collaborating directly in the generation of wealth and local environmental preservation, with direct benefits to the performer, in a B2P modality.

The INEPP, sponsor of the technology of Amazonascoin and Amazonas Token, as an OSCIP accredited by the Ministry of Justice, gathers the necessary conditions, immediately, to receive the resources of several governmental and non-governmental funds and to start the projects of certification of carbon credits and financing for sustainable extractive rubber exploration and processing of chestnuts, as well as other projects in the educational area, generation of solar energy and / or biomass and replanting of the degraded regions with syringe or chestnut seedlings.

Landowners and riverside communities will be able to receive, directly, via AMAZONASCOIN (open blockchain technology – AMZ or permitted blockchain technology – AMT), with security, transparency, and anti-fraud monitoring, with direct benefits, based on the existence and maintenance of seringueiras (rubber trees) and castanheiras (chestnut trees) in their areas, generating an opportunity to generate income with preservation.

The Amazon region is known for the difficulty of logistics. The logistics of taking fiduciary money (paper) is also hampered by the lack of roads and the high cost of air transportation. It is estimated that each R$ 1.00 transported to isolated locations, costs approximately R$ 10.00.

The crypto digital bank system can be installed in all businesses in any municipality in the interior of Amazonas, whether for payments or withdrawals. This will increase purchasing power, as it will reduce the need for paper circulation and the bureaucratic process of opening bank accounts at banks in the region. The region has immense difficulty in receiving paper money and its respective withdrawal.

Amazonas Token will be traded on the Decentralized Exchange architecture – DEX within the scope of Permitted Blockchain – POP, with international reach and, in addition to B2B, will be the first in the world to have a P2B, B2P and P2P reach, eliminating the intermediaries to increase the speed of receipt of resources by the end-user. The system is anti-fraud because it is fully traceable via blockchain and runs via smart contract from Amazonascoin – AMZ and / or Amazonastoken – AMT technology.

The needy populations will have the possibility to receive the resources destined to them, minimizing the number of intermediaries between the availability of the resource and its use, being able to carry out payment processes in real-time.

They may be able to receive financial resources regardless of the bureaucracy of opening bank accounts through an application of a crypto digital bank, a smart way to reach out to unbanked people and people not registered in the available social programs.

Associations or cooperatives may participate in a productive activity such as "crypto mining." Crypto mining was recognized as a productive activity that should be included in countries' trade scales, according to the World Bank's recommendation. The Central Bank of Brazil already follows this recommendation.

Innovative Potential

Finally, commodity tokenization, as a voluntary or imposing environmental offsetting asset, carries with it the potential to be an innovative and valuable crypto asset for the 2020-22 biennium; it is an asset with exponential possibilities and financial and non-financial gains and benefits.

It is a smart way to use the digital economy in a reliable, transparent, flexible, scalable way and with a massive transformational purpose aligned with the goals of the millennium, and capable of being associated with the maximum number of people and companies and still creating a community, a real crowd of followers.

The way the digital economy equips an ecosystem based on the tokenization of commodities and the collateralization of a crypto asset with the same commodities, such as carbon credit, makes it complete. In addition to being able to produce smart contracts and issue tokens based on real assets, it can be acquired simultaneously with its speculative digital asset.

The purpose and architecture of its collaborative fund is a powerful catalyst for solid investors and a source of sustainability for a better world. After all, the 21st century belongs to men, women, and companies that will make a difference, transforming the world into a better version so that our children and grandchildren can prosper.

Chapter 10

Blockchain in Agribusiness

Cryptocurrencies: The money of the future

For one of the most important and wealth-generating sectors of Brazil's economy, the Agribusiness, Blockchain, has a huge advantage that lies in the reliability of the data available on shared networks.

With the blockchain, it is possible, for example, to share information with different agents involved in a production chain, from planting to sale on supermarket shelves, providing a total tracking of a product in a safe, decentralized, immutable, encrypted and flexible way.

All this with the possibility of tracing and tracking the entire production process, in distribution, commercialization, export, and monetization, considering that the market already recognizes the present and future production of Agribusiness in its broadest verticalization as physical assets that can be easily transformed into digital assets and operated on various exchanges and exchanges of digital assets in Brazil and worldwide.

One of the recent examples of a Brazilian Agribusiness image crisis could be avoided if blockchain was already in operation in the sector: Operation Carne Fraca, named by the Federal Police on less than 0.5% of Brazilian meatpackers that acted illegal, but it seems that in Brazil its whole meat production, did not comply with regular sanitary requirements.

If food traceability mechanisms were widespread in the national meat industry, and this should happen in all other sectors of the Agribusiness Industry, quickly all rumors would be eliminated, and the correct processes disclosed, avoiding an international crisis and losses throughout the production chain.

In this context, we are participating in an extraordinary project under development with rural producers from the Brazilian states of Mato Grosso, Mato Grosso do Sul and Goias, called Agribusiness Coin - ABC, which is a crypto asset 100% developed by entrepreneurs, producers and specialists in Blockchain and Digital Economy, all Brazilian.

Besides, the entire process is being done with the adoption of Native Blockchain, based on the proof of Consensus PoCP – Proof of Capacity Permitted, with the most ecological data mining system (cyber mining) considered the most ecological and correctly environmental mining technology of all the Blockchain ecosystem, which allows for greater decentralization with minimal cost of natural resources, since it uses approximately 1/500 fraction of the energy consumed in other consensus proofs of other Blockchain in the market, such as POW and POS for example.

This initiative of the Crypto Asset of Agribusiness is intended, in harmony with another action described previously, which would be the Crypto Asset of Environmental Preservation and Recovery, (amazonascoin) a peaceful, harmonious, friendly and optimizing, with economic, environmental, climate and social result.

This could be possible, considering that the Agribusiness sector itself with the Environmental sector, together, can establish metrics and compensatory values to promote the sustainable economic developm e nt of Agribusiness, with investments an d waivers of part of its digital assets rep r esentative, to apply to projects for the preservation, recovery, expansion, and improvement of the climate and environmental impacts in each nat i on, always respecting their sovereignty and independence.

In practice, both sectors could c o ntinue to share initiatives that contrib u te to the balance of sustainable developmen t   with environmental preservation, especially with transparent and public actions registered and with the respective crypto assets monetized and compensated via Blockchain, without intermediaries, with absolute self-regulation, regardless of taxation and tax waivers in favor of this harmony promoted by the State.

Chapter 11

Blockchain in Government – GovTech / GovChain

GovTech" or "GovChain" is the term used to refer to innovative and potentially disruptive technologies, in particular Blockchain technology – for use by the public sector and third sector institutions to improve the management and transparency of public and fiscal resources.

Governments globally struggle with embezzlement, fraud, waste, abuse, and mismanagement of government resources, usually due to inefficiencies in outdated, disparate, or multiple systems, created in favor of bureaucracy, which always aims to sell hardship and buy ease.

Government pain points include slow and complicated records and transfers of data and transactions, limited access to asset liquidity and property transfers, significant payment delays due to reconciliations and ineffective tracking of assets and purchasing services, favoring acts and practices of active and passive corruption at all levels and expectations of the Government and also in the third sector supplied with public and fiscal resources.

This initiative allows the government, in all its levels and powers, giving the example of the Federal Executive Branch, to make public management directly, indirectly, autarchic and foundational, more efficient, responsive and extremely capable of serving society more digital intelligence and less bureaucracy and regulation, more efficiency and results, in its management processes and attention to citizens in their effectively essential needs owed by the State, with lower costs and agility in public services.

GovTech / GovChain will significantly improve the transparency of the entire transaction generation, registration, and recording process – including digitally signed smart contracts and simplified, integrated, absolutely secure and tamper-proof, and unalterable identification verification.

It also makes it possible to inform the modeling of current and new digital assets, crypto assets or cryptocurrencies, in public and auditable digital ratio, and the impact that digital currencies would have on the monetary supply and monetary policy of the Central Bank.

It also makes it possible for all Data Mining carried out by crypto assets in Brazil, to be appropriated and recorded in the country's trade balance, improving the

Central Bank's balance sheet indexes. It also provides that a single immutable record visible only to the relevant counterparties for a transaction or recurring transactions, adapting to decentralized, permitted, or public architectures, with public or private reading, with public or private writing, or even distributed.

The recommended blockchain at the level of GovTech / GovChain and E-Nations would be with the proof of consensus PoP – Proof of Participation with the Permissioned chain, where the reading will be public, but the writing is private, controlled although decentralized.

BLOCKCHAIN applied in Seborga E-Principality, extended to other Micro United Nations

The Principality of Seborga fully enters the Digital Economy, establishes its supreme national economic and crypto-monetary agenda as of 2020, this being yet another project that I am honored to be a consultant and collaborating proponent for the creation of a new Micro Digital Economy 100% based on Blockchain to serve the Principality of Seborga in its status as National Supra Nation, and the other Micro United Nations in the world, recognized or not recognized by other nations / states.

Luigi and Luigino Coin – Seborga's Crypto Assets for the inclusion and integration of Micro United Nations in the digital economy, with the purpose of becoming a new Economic Crypto Block in this new digital economy, to include micro-nations, peoples and economies that are practically nonexistent or precarious, most of them played their luck in isolated, remote areas and without any support, recognition and many of them without opportunities to establish their economic and financial independence and autonomy, although some already possess territorial sovereignty.

The Principality of Seborga under the current administration of Prince Nicolas First, through its Special Delegation of the Principality of Seborga formally established in Brazil, duly registered as an international body governed by public law, with the status of Special Diplomatic Delegation in Brazil, established development agreements, cooperation, and pacts with private and third sector bodies.

These agreements are intended to receive technical support and specialized human resources to consolidate their project to build a 100% supra national nation, with supranational currency and strengthen their goal of becoming a Blockchain Nation – Supra National, with digital residents and entrepreneurs in the new digital economy using its Permitted Blockchain that will serve Micro Nations around the world.

Seborga, when creating its promising new digital economy based 100% on its e-principality, constitutes itself for the world as a Blockchain Nation, where everything will work and will be registered, controlled, audited and decentralized through Blockchain and its explorer, including its certificates, digital identity, public and private documents, and including the global third sector licensed by Seborga.

In this way, it will expand its sovereignty and presence as a nation, economy and supranational currency, constituting bilateral and multilateral agreements with countries on European, African, Latin American and other continents, establishing chambers of commerce and technology as the commercial and technological hub of its digital economy, based on native Blockchain, with consensus proof called PoP – Proof of Participation, and its data mining with Permitted License, totally ecological called VirtualMining – EVM.

Seborga defines the purpose for this new economy, not only to benefit Seborga's territory, which is still unrecognized and with a lot of folklore and monarchs who are self-declared sovereign princes, likewise the objective is not only to benefit their few and current residents but to create a new economic-social block to benefit all micronations and their respective citizens and residents around the world, regardless of their size, status and recognition.

It is intended to install and host in Seborga, an International Organization for the Micro United Nations, aiming not only to bring economic, financial, monetary, social, educational, cultural, assistance benefits, but also to develop and implement public security policies, of personal development, professional and business in the scope of digital transformation, as well as prevention and care actions in the area of health, sanitation, social and digital inclusion, a n d also, generation of job opportunities, incom e with production and distribution of wealth t h at only a new 100% digital, inclusive and s u pranational economy would be able to produce.

Seborga also, through it s Special Delegation in Brazil, si g ned a technical, institutional and public interest cooperation agreement with the Natio n al Institute of Public

Policy Excellence – INEPP, a civil society organization of public interest, accredited by Federal Law 9.790 / 90 by the Ministry of Justice and Public Security of Brazil, to establish in Seborga the world headquarters for the Organization of the Micro United Nations.

It is a Technological HUB and a multi-lateral Blockchain Lab, from Brazil, which is one of the most evolved countries in experiences with disruptive technologies, in particular Blockchain, Artificial Intelligence, IOT – Internet of Things, robotics, sustainable energy, environment, agribusiness, and others, considering the expertise that INEPP accumulates in this new Crypto Economy through its International Disruptive Technology Agency.

Through this same organization – INEPP, and under the same Cooperation term, the Principality of Seborga, through its Special Delegation in Brazil, and with its natural vocation and concern for environmental and climate issues in the world, decided to unconditionally support another project of a 100% Brazilian and native Crypto Asset, which is Amazonascoin, whose crypto crowdfunding is managed by INEPP.

Amazonascoin constitutes the crypto asset of environmental preservation, conservation, and recovery, diagnosing and certifying private consigned areas, with its own methodology for accounting and carrying out environmental compensations in areas intended for preservation, through INEPP, with the Amazonascoin project, headquartered in the municipality of Barcelos, in the state of Amazonas.

In this sense, Seborga decides to list this Amazonascoin – AMZ asset on its digital assets stock exchange, Seborga Stock Exchange, and also on its digital platform – CryptoTECH – Seborga Digital Bank, within the scope of its Treasury Department and Central Digital Bank, to exchange AMZ with the legal digital currency of Seborga, SPL (Luigino Coin).

Also through the OSCIP – INEPP agreements and technologies, the Principality of Seborga, through its Special Delegation in Brazil, also established within the scope of its e-principality, the global blockchain digital platform license and the Digital Platform for a university of human development, empowerment and social therapy, called Human Empowerment University.

Likewise, to start its operations, to apply self-knowledge diagnostics and talent detection, compared with a professional profile in more than 700 careers and vocational guidance for young people and adults, in addition to developing smart training programs, identifying and mapping the star of the social and behavioral identity;

Also, providing a 24-hour online coach through the Empowerment Systems platform, that is developed through artificial intelligence and specialized systems, even allowing the application of methodologies for Social and Behavioral Therapy.

The Seborga Special Delegation will also offer free courses and professional training and specialization at the first moment, advancing at undergraduate, master's and doctoral level, through the Royal University of Seborga, benefiting all current and future citizens and residents of the supra-national nation of Seborga, extended to the citizens of the Micro United Nations.

Finally, through INEPP, within the scope of its INEPP duties and powers, it will allocate up to 25% of all production of the PoC – Proof of Capacity crypto asset called Amazonascoin – AMZ, and will award up to 25% of all production of the stable crypto asset Amazonas Token – AMT, from its data mining with Permissioned license, totally ecological called Eco Virtual Mining, via EVM, supported with the crypto crowdfunding managed by INEPP.

With this plan, the Principality of Seborga through the Special Delegation of the Principality of Seborga in Brazil, with its agreements and partnerships, and the crypto assets Luigi, Luigino Coin, Amazonascoin and Emerald Cash, starts its supra-national operations from its Special Delegation constituted in Brazil, and soon, with Special Delegations established in other countries and continents that come to support the economic and social development plan of Seborga and the Micro United Nations.

http://www.principautedeseborga.com

www.luiginocoin.com

www.gemstonebrasil.com

www.seborgastockexchange.com

www.inepp.org.br

www.humanempowermentuniversity.com

www.principadodeseborga.org

www.cryptotech.com.br

BLOCKCHAIN applied in E-Nation (Digital Nation)

Estonia, Government in the Clouds

Estonia was a pioneer in converting public services into flexible electronic solutions for its electronic citizens and residents. The implementation of the Government Cloud solution provides an excellent basis for public electronic services and solutions, making Estonia the most digital country in the world. With the Government Cloud solution, Estonia is taking the next step in its digital evolution to expand its digital society.

The Estonian government's super cloud will lead to the modernization and renewal of existing information systems, to take advantage of the opportunities offered by cloud technology, and allow more agility in the provision of electronic services by Estonian government agencies and critical service providers to residents and e-residents.

The solution will help integrate IT infrastructure into existing Estonian public sector silos in a shared pool of resources. Estonian public institutions will gradually move from existing legacy systems to a new Government Cloud solution, which has been developed according to the national IT security standard (ISKE), to ensure compliance with security and quality requirements. For example, sensitive personal data is stored and handled with confidentiality and integrity.

To accommodate physical security requirements, the Estonian Government Cloud will be deployed in two locations, one outside the capital. This will allow the management of data and information systems in a distributed manner. To support Estonia's "digital" independence and the uninterrupted operation of public IT services in a state of emergency, there is a long-term plan to establish electronic embassies outside Estonia in friendly foreign countries.

GovTech in Canada

The Government of Canada (GC) is using blockchain technology to send to project-based employees a type of digital resume, providing "a permanent, independent and secure record of their skills and experiences."

Alex Benay, the country's chief information officer, announced the project last week in a blog post, writing: "Proving with paper or checking a database will now be a thing of the past."

The project team will receive digital credentials called Blockcerts. These will be recognized and accepted by the government's experimental jobs platform, Talent Cloud.

Case of concrete blockchain use in Canada

At the Digital 9 Summit in November 2018, the intention of exploring a pilot for Blockchain credentials was shared with the Massachusetts Institute of Technology (MIT). Since then, MIT Media Lab, together with [Machine Technology] Learning Machine, has developed an open international standard for issuing digital credentials known as Blockcerts.

Since 2016, the Government of Canada has been experimenting with a new model of workforce that aims to provide a flexible and adaptable workforce, suited to 21st-century public services. Floating government officials, known as "Free Agents," were hired to work on short-term projects at various public sector agencies.

Liechtenstein enters the blockchain and token world

Liechtenstein defines new regulation for tokens, virtual assets, and blockchain service providers. The Liechtenstein government announced that it passed a new regulation for tokenization on May 8, 2019.

According to the statement, the new Token and VT Service Providers Act seeks to improve investor protection, combat money laundering, and offer more clarity. Tokenized assets are mentioned in the regulation and how digital token systems can be used to tokenize real-world assets.

The number of blockchain companies continues to grow also in Switzerland, which has already regulated this activity and today grants licenses for Cryptocurrencies, Exchange, and Crypto Banks.

AFRA / DIGITAL AFRICAN CENTRAL BANK / SAPA

The AFRA System – African Finance Regulatory Authority, in the digital sphere, and the African Central Bank (ACB) in Blockchain, with the creation of the African Continent Legal Course Currency called AFRA Coin, is one of the five original financial institutions and specialized agencies of African Union. Over time, it will be able to assume the responsibilities of the African Monetary Crypto Fund.

The creation of the ACB (African Central Bank on Blockchain), which is already partially implemented and should be completed in 2020/2021, started a pilot project in May 2015 under the exclusive supervision of the AFRA Commission, the African Finance Regulatory Authority. The AFRA Commission mandate is guided by Article 19 of the OAU Constitutive Law, by the Abuja Treaty of 1991, and as agreed by the Assembly of Member States for the Single AFRA Payments Area (SAPA), the economic and crypto monetary systems and the creation of African Central Bank (ACB) on Blockchain, charged by the African Finance Regulatory Authority.

The African Star Treaty Alliance Group, declared by the FOURTH EXTRAORDINARY SESSION OF THE ASSEMBLY OF HEADS OF STATE AND GOVERNMENT of the Organization of African Unity, 1999, in Sirte, Libya.

When fully implemented, ACB will be the sole issuer of the single cryptocurrency on the African continent, called AFRA COIN and will be the Digital Central Bank of the African continent, being the continental crypto banker, which will regulate and supervise the African cryptocurrency or crypto assets sector and define the currency parity policies, exchange rates, and official rates; together with the administration of African governments that are members of AFRA and shareholders of BCA and SAPA

The African Financial Regulatory Authority Commission (AFRA) is the statutory body mandated by the African Union Heads of State and Government for the legal instruments of the Treaty, referred to as ASTAG since its creation in 1999, in the Sirte Declaration, after the Abuja Treaty of 1991, currently with the new digital economy dedicated to crypto economic and monetary crypto purposes, with the union of member countries for the incorporation of its continental cryptocurrency called AFRA COIN.

This is another project that I am honored to participate as a consultant, collaborator and proponent for the creation of the new digital crypto-economy for the African continent, through the already established ecosystem called AFRA / BCA / SAPA, where we have already built the Afra Coin Blockchain, its Digital Crypto Assets Exchange, its Data Mining Permitted (Cyber Mining), using the Blockchain and Consensus Proof PoCP – Proof of Capacity Permitted, its Blo c kchain explorer, and the Technology is read y to issue smart contracts and tokenize commo d ities and other financial assets, real state, security and utilities from participating member countries, under the AFRA / BCA / SAPA system.

https://afracoin.africa/

https://www.acb.africa/

www.popblockchain.org

Chapter 12

Blockchain Security and Reliability

Is blockchain a secure and inviolable platform?

As a database, compared to others hosted in the cloud, Blockchain is not the fastest. It is also not the one with the highest number of transactions per second. However, it has the great advantage of not having an administrator. On the contrary, it is distributed over thousands of servers, with a "mirror mode" system that replicates information across all other data centers around the world. Thus, the burden of responsibility is not just on a single entity.

It is a system for validating chain transactions, encrypted and decentralized, which makes the platform inviolable. In short, why is it safe? Very simple, the security guarantee is given by encryption. Access to data is done only from a private key and through the distribution and replication of data, as we have already seen.

In short, its security lies in the fact that in order to have a change in one of the servers, all the others will have to agree to that change, which would not happen due to its decentralized and verifying nature.

Is anonymity ensured for commercial transactions to be made in a 100% digital currency?

There is no guarantee of anonymity in accessing and sharing data through the technology that supports cryptocurrencies using Exchanges to trade digital assets. The blockchain is an immutable / unalterable platform, and you cannot delete, replace, or change registered and verified data.

We have to demystify blockchain and cryptocurrencies by humanizing these expressions and their relationship with the market and ordinary users.

In these last ten years of experience with this new crypto-economy in full consolidation, it is necessary to understand that this is not an experiment. This thinking is no longer valid. Crypto-economy has reached substantial maturity, and the issue is no longer a myth.

This last decade gives us a meaningful and relevant background in the world economy, the proof of this is the vast number of Governments, Central Banks, Companies, and Organizations with and without profit purposes, including the IMF itself.

Even the International Monetary Fund (IMF), seen by many as the enslaver of a segregating Monetary Policy and which has taken hostage all underdeveloped countries and peoples, and also some developing countries, is currently studying the adoption of blockchain technology, with the aim of perpetuating its current international monetary policy, although considered by many to be perverse, but perhaps changing the form (format), but maintaining the essence.

Only with the characteristics of this new market for crypto assets, will it be able to free the governments and their people from this perverse monetary policy in force, generating independence, the inclusion of their digital assets in fair and more equal conditions in several exchanges spread around the world.

The evolution of this new crypto-economy, partially or even entirely, would be a way to free these hostage countries from the burden of foreign debt and to resolve their domestic debts with independence and social justice, in order to generate development, wealth and, of course, the distribution of these riches to their people.

Many countries will even be able to support their future crypto assets with their mineral and natural wealth, which would naturally add enormous value and wealth to their respective digital assets. This is because fiduciary currencies today do not bring any kind of support, but the value that the state attributes to them, that is, we would be going back to the origins, taking advantage of the enormous technological evolution that we have experienced.

Worldwide, the regions where this technology is already a comprehensive reality are Asia (Japan, China, and South Korea), Australia and part of the USA, Canada, Mexico, Europe, and Latin America, in particular, Brazil.

Chapter 13

Crypto Dictionary – Terms and Expressions used in Crypto Economics and Blockchain

Altcoins – Also called alternative currencies and referred to all virtual currencies and tokens that emerged after the creation of Bitcoin. Apart from Bitcoin, all other currencies are called AltCoins.

AML – (Anti-Money Laundering), techniques used to try to prevent money laundering. In Brazil, some brokers already investigate the origin of funds when the value of a transaction is very high.

Arbitration – A strategy in which a person buys certain crypto from an exchange that is at the lowest price and sells it at another exchange that is at the highest price.

ASIC – (Application Specific Integrated Circuit), it is a chip created to perform a specific task. In the case of Bitcoin, it was designed to process the SHA – 256 hash.

ATH – (All-Time High), indicates that the price of virtual currency has reached the highest rate in history.

ATM – (Automated Teller Machine). They allow their users to make purchases and sales of Bitcoins and some AltCoins, using credit cards, debit cards, and also fiduciary money.

Attack of 51% – It is when a person or a group can dominate the computational power of more than 51% of the computers of the network. The purpose of this would be to have control of the blockchain to be able to make some kind of profit by making changes in transactions, for example.

Bear – It is the way investors who are pessimistic about the market are called.

Bear Market – Term used to express that the market is down, which is when prices are falling.

Bitcoin – Like Real and Dollar, Bitcoin is a currency. The difference is that it is entirely virtual. Created in 2008, its main feature is its system that is 100% decentralized, known as peer-to-peer, which enables to make transactions without the need for intermediaries.

Blockchain – The technology behind Bitcoin and all other AltCoins. It functions as a ledger that records all the transactions made on the Bitcoin network and others. It forms a continuous chain of hash (transaction receipts) verified by the network itself, composing a unique record that cannot be modified.

To ensure that your system is secure since the blockchain does not need intermediaries to function, all computers connected to it have a copy of the blockchain information. Even if a person tries to change the data, it will not affect the system, since all other computers have real information.

Block explorer – A website that allows the user to consult details about generated blocks, transactions made, addresses, and other information about the blockchain.

Blockchain.info – A site that offers its users the service of creating a virtual wallet and also access to information about the blocks of Bitcoin – BTC blockchain.

BTC – Abbreviation of Bitcoin.

Bull – the so-called "bulls" are investors who believe that there will be an increase in the price of an asset.

Bull Market – Term used to represent an upward trend in prices in the market.

Cold wallet – The offline wallet is considered the safest way to store your crypto since it is not connected to the internet.

Confirmation – The process of confirming a transaction is carried out only by the miners (computers with high processing capacity). They verify, validate and publish all valid transactions on the blockchain. A transaction can only be considered confirmed when all this process is completed.

Confirmations – A transaction is confirmed when it is added to a valid block. After another block is added to the network, after the first one, the transaction will have two confirmations, and so on. Confirmations can only be done by miners.

Cryptocurrencies – It is the name given to virtual currencies that, like any other currency, have buying and selling power in the market. They became known by this name because they use encryption to guarantee security and preserve the information of their users.

Crypto Leasing – Lease System for crypto assets generally offered by Crypto Licensed Banks or Exchange of Crypto Assets that operate in the Crypto Trade market with their own desk.

dApps – Term used to refer to decentralized applications.

Day trader – It is a strategy used by investors with a bolder profile. Traders are looking to buy and sell on the same day for a quick profit.

Decentralized – A decentralized system does not need intermediaries to function.

DEX – Exchange Decentralized based on P2P platforms – Person to Person, with a Stable Coin stable parity, which eliminates the use of Brokers or Stock Exchanges with a database and Centralized Custody.

Digital Assets – this term is used to refer to any crypto or token, including Bitcoin – BTC.

Double spending – It is when trying to spend twice the same amount. One of the mathematical problems in achieving a secure virtual currency was preventing someone from spending the same money twice. Because of it, Satoshi Nakamoto came up with the idea of using the mining process to resolve this issue.

These machines with high processing capacity (miners) have the function of verifying, confirming, and publishing on the blockchain all transactions that take place within the Bitcoin network. In this way, double spending is avoided.

Dump – Term used to refer to a sudden drop in the price of crypto.

Exchanges – The exchanges, or cryptocurrency brokers, act as intermediaries for the purchase and sale of digital currencies and store the currencies in the clients' wallets, keeping them in custody online or offline.

Fees – For each trade that takes place on the blockchain, you will have to pay a fee for it.

FIAT currency – These are the well-known fiduciary currencies, which are regulated and controlled by a central government.

FOMO – "Fear Of Missing Out" or "fear of missing an opportunity." It's what you feel when an asset is growing in value, and everyone is buying, except you. Beware of this trap: better stay out than to buy only high values.

Forks – Forks are updates to the protocol or code of a particular crypto asset. When there is no consensus in the community on which way to go, a fork and a new cryptocurrency are usually generated. The primary examples are Litecoin and Bitcoin Cash that are Bitcoin forks.

FUD – (Fear, uncertainty, and doubt). Generally, this feeling occurs when the market experiences large price drops, or when it becomes stagnant.

Full Node – Also known as full validating nodes are essential computer programs to keep, for example, the Bitcoin network and other cryptocurrency networks functioning properly.

They have the role of checking independently if the rules of the system are being followed. This is only possible because each time a miner transmits a block, the full nodes analyze whether the information contained is correct, and if the system rules are followed if any attempt is made by miners to circumvent the standards, full nodes can reject the block.

GAS – In the Ethereum network, gas is a computational work measurement unit. It is through it that it is analyzed how much "fuel" will be needed to perform a specific operation. The higher the computational strength is for a transaction to take place, the higher its value.

GAS LIMIT – Total amount of "gas" that a transaction can consume.

GAS PRICE – It is related to how much Ethereum a user intends to pay for his transaction to take place. In other Altcoins, other nomenclatures are adopted.

The time limit for a transaction to be completed is directly linked to the amount paid. So, if someone is in a hurry and wants their transaction to be confirmed faster, they must pay more for it.

Genesis block – It is how the first block of a blockchain is called.

GPU – (Graphical Processing Unit). It is a chip whose function is to process complex mathematical calculations used in the protocol of Bitcoin, its forks, and other AltCoins.

Halving – Periodic event that consists of reducing the reward paid to miners by 50% for their work, and considerably increases the processing capacity and infrastructure for mining.

Hard Forks – It is a fork mode. In the hard fork, there is a break with the past rules; there is a change in the rules of operation of the currency. With this, each created block will be published in a new blockchain, which follows the changes made to the rules, however, the old determination still exist, and are worth the previous version.

Hash – The hash is a summary of the transactions that occurred in a block. Represented by a sequence of letters and numbers, it serves as a "fingerprint" of each mined block.

Hashpower – It is the ability of a computer to mine new blocks.

Hashrate – (Computational power). It is the number of hashes that a computer is capable of mining in a period of time.

Hash rate – It is a measure of processing power. This rate measures how many attempts the network can make to solve the complex mathematical calculation (hash).

HODL – Derived from the word "hold," hodl, (yes, the D is before the L) is an abbreviation of the expression Hold On For Dear Life, which refers to holding the cryptocurrency rather than selling it, expecting a great appreciation.

Hodl or Hold – (Hold on for dear life). Act to keep a coin without caring about the price.

Hot Wallet – A wallet is considered "hot" when its private key is on a computer or a website.

Hype – This term is used to say that something is a trend, or that it is the focus of attention.

ICO – Initial Coin Offering. It is a process used to raise funds to develop a particular project.

Immutability – In the cryptocurrency market, immutability means that once a mined block is published on the blockchain, all transactions within can no longer be changed. This factor is essential to guarantee the security and trust of those who negotiate some type of crypto.

Input – Term used for entering transactions at an address.

Kilohashes / sec – KH/S – Number of attempts that can be made to resolve a hash per second, measured in thousands of hashes.

KYC – Know Your Customer. These are measures taken by financial institutions to find out who their customers are.

KYC – Know Your Customer, identification, recognition, and verification processes of the client, or KYB – Know your Business, also to establish processes of identification, recognition, and verification of client companies.

Ledger – Distributed ledger. A term used to explain how Blockchain works.

Lending – It means lending your crypto to generate profits through daily interest.

Libra – Virtual currency of the social network Facebook.

Liquidity – Volume of money available to execute orders in the market.

Long – It is a strategy used by investors who decide to buy coins because they believe their market value will rise.

Mão de alface – An expression in Portuguese meaning **Lettuce Hands**, famous in Brazilian soccer and introduced into the universe of digital coins, meaning a person who cannot live with the volatility of the cryptocurrencies and, at the first sign of decrease, simply give up on them.

microbit-uBTC – It is the millionth part of a Bitcoin (0.000001 BTC)

miliBit-mBTC – It is the thousandth part of a Bitcoin (0.001 BTC = 1 mBTC)

Mining – It is a process that consists of verifying, confirming, and publishing valid Bitcoin and other Altcoin transactions on the blockchain. It aims to ensure that they occur safely, without currency being sent more than once, as it is a chain of blocks of transaction / record / transaction, for the rest of the network know about it, and it is used to distinguish legitimate Bitcoins and AltCoins transactions from attempts of reusing the currencies.

Multiple Signature – (multi-sig), it is a feature that allows a cryptocurrency to be spent only if a group of people authorizes the transaction. Companies generally use this type of function to prevent expenses made without the consent of all members who have the key to the wallet.

Nodes – It is the way we call computers that download software from virtual currency to participate in the network (Bitcoin, Ethereum, among others).

Open protocol – The protocol of Bitcoin, Ethereum, and other cryptocurrencies is published openly so that it is possible to review the code of these cryptos, suggest changes, and also create improvements. However, for any decision to implement something new to be taken, a network consensus is required.

Order maker – It is the process of creating an order at the broker. This happens when a person wants to buy cryptocurrencies, but the desired amount is not available at that time.

Order taker – Term used to indicate that a buying or selling crypto order will be executed immediately.

Output – Represent the outputs of a wallet.

Peer-to-peer (P2P) – In this system, transactions can be made directly from one person to another (peer-to-peer) without the need to do business with an intermediary, like a bank or central server.

Pool (mining pool) – Are formed by groups of miners who "add" their computational power. It aims to find a faster way to solve the complex mathematical calculation, and thus earn the reward in cryptocurrency.

This way, despite decreasing the profit of each miner that will be proportional to the contribution made by him, the gains will be more frequent since the chance of being able to mine alone is much less.

Private key – It is the code that allows the user to access their virtual cryptocurrency wallet as if it was the password of a bank account.

Proof of Capacity (PoC) – It is a type of mining less known. It uses spaces on the HD of the miner's computer as proof of capacity. Whoever has more space available on the HD is more likely to be the creator of the next block.

Proof of Participation (PoP) – This type of mining does not need investing in physical infrastructure or computer power. Its transactions are made practically in an instant, and basically free of charge, generally adopted in the B2B or I2I market, in addition to the adoption in GovChain projects.

Proof of Stake (PoS) – This type of mining does not need computational power to solve the algorithm. A random draw is made to define who will be the creator of the next block. An important factor for this type of mining is having assets in hands because whoever has more coins is more likely to be the chosen miner.

Proof of Work (PoW) – As the name implies, PoW is proof that a job has been done. This verification is done by the miners that spend all the resources of their machines to solve complex mathematical calculations, in order to confirm and publish transactions in a block on the blockchain.

Public key – Also known as asymmetric cryptography, it is any cryptographic system that uses keys in pairs: public keys can be widely disseminated and private keys that are known only to its owner.

Pump – When the price of an asset is rising too fast. The opposite of this is *dump*. The term pump-dump is used to refer to market manipulation.

QR Code – It is a two-dimensional bar code used as an address for each person's virtual wallet.

Rekt – Expression that means "to be totally destroyed or ruined" and is used when investors have lost much of what they had after a sudden change in the market price.

Satoshi – Considered the smallest fraction of a Bitcoin (0.00000001 BTC).

Scam – Sites that make tempting proposals to take advantage of a person making some kind of profit.

ScamCoin – AltCoin created with the purpose of scamming its users and enriching its creators.

Segregated Witness (SegWit) – SegWit is an update proposed by Bitcoin Core to correct the problem of transaction malleability and network scalability. For this update to be possible, it was necessary to separate the digital signature data for each BTC transaction on the blockchain.

Taking into account that the size of each Bitcoin is 1 MB, in making this change, more space was available with the blocks, making more room for new transactions.

Smart Contract – It is a self-executing computer protocol, created to allow people who do not know each other to negotiate safely, without the need for intermediaries.

Spread – It is the difference between the buy (demand) and sells (offer) price of a share or a currency.

STO – Security Token Offering. It is a process used to raise funds to develop a particular project.

Stop-Limit – It is a programmed order where it is possible to buy or sell crypto when it reaches the price that the user has chosen. Stop: When the currency reaches the value X. Limit: add a purchase order (you can choose which amount you would like to buy).

Supply – It is the total amount of coins that will be made available on the market.

Swing Trader – It is an operational strategy of buying an asset to obtain profit in the short term.

Token – It is the representation of an asset. A token can represent a percentage of a company, an asset, an acquired right, or it can also be used as money within a given platform.

ToTheMoon – Expression used to indicate that the value of the currency is rising.

Trader – Investor and / or operator whose objective is to make money with short-term operations, taking advantage of market volatility.

Transaction fee (Mining fee) – Fee paid to miners when making a transaction.

Txid (Transaction ID) – Number generated as a form of receipt every time a transaction occurs.

Volatility – It is a way of measuring the change in the value of a currency; The greater the variation in the price of an asset in a short period of time, the greater the volatility.

Wallets – Crypto asset "wallets" is software used to manage the address and private key, allowing you to receive, send, and consultation of the bitcoin balance.

Whale – People who have large amounts of cryptocurrencies. "Whales" can influence the market when they sell their crypto assets.

White Paper – It is a document written by a developer. It presents an idea or a new concept.

CONCLUSION
Experience and Legacy

So, I conclude this material with a few words about my experience of many years working in this field. I begin by saying that the secret of success is to broaden the vision and see the disruptive movements, and anticipate the future, be bold but prudent, be aggressive, but cautious, be visionary, but rational, be intuitive, but realistic.

I also tell you that an authentic entrepreneur needs to take risks to experience success. Likewise, you need to know how to manage eventual failures and defeats, not letting yourself be shaken and seeking in the bad experiences: wisdom, strength, and determination to, if necessary, start all over again, from scratch, without caring about the opinions of the experts who never did what you did, as they would never do, because fear and excessive conservatism won't allow them to do it.

These negative and overly conservative people cannot serve as examples for you; seek to mirror those who have experienced failure, but have overcome and are now successful. If you want to be a lion, do not walk with a cat, cats walk with cats and lions walk with lions, (quote from my friend and Pastor Glaybson Silva, from the Evangelical Community of Miami - CEM, author of Building Strong Relationships), and be inspired by success stories, not circumstances of failure.

For a true entrepreneur, failures are only circumstances, since success is the target and will always be the finish line of a born entrepreneur, determined and aware of his role in society and purpose in this world aligned with the spiritual world, and notably social responsibility, where the wealth generated by his enterprise can benefit people, families and future generations.

Remember that success is not merely a common result, accessible to everyone and anyone, but a consequence of your effort, work, determination and ability to overcome challenges, just as prosperity is not a right or a privilege, but a blessing to those who strive, are disciplined, determined, bold and confident in biblical teachings and also in secular lessons and experiences.

When you want to follow someone's steps, always focus on someone who has already fallen before rising, so as not to follow someone who is still standing, but has not yet fallen and will certainly fall, because real learning comes with real-world practice, not just theory.

As much as we have theoretical foundations, the experience is what creates the proper conditions to achieve success and complete happiness, which is not only money but personal, professional, business, and Christian fulfillment.

Your enterprise can help change society, the world and, in our example, digital finances, the private monetary system, with the new crypto-economy and the new generation of personal, professional, corporate and governmental wealth, for the benefit of the individual and not for the great economic groups dominating and centralizing. That is the vast legacy that we leave in this world.

The disruption today comes to change the accommodating and centralizing financial system and the capital market system to remove them from the comfort zone, which can knock them down and leave them stunned with innovation, security, simplicity, and decentralization. Today this movement is irreversible, at least in the financial sector and the new digital economy.

No one accepts a financial institution leveraging its capital and assets anymore, preventing you from using its money regarding how, when, and where it wants you to take it. This is the real strength of Digital Disruption brought by Blockchain Technology, which is already changing the old, outdated and costly world of fiduciary finance, the current forced-currency monetary system, and the complex and closed capital market which only enriches a handful of privileged individuals.

I dream of soon seeing digital change and transformation taking place in the poor and underdeveloped countries, corrupted and enslaved by their cruel, authoritarian rulers and dictators, like on the African continent, and also a transformation by the new digital economy in the micro-nations, regardless of their degree of recognition.

I dare to believe in the end, or the drastic decrease in corruption rates, especially in the countries of South and Central America, following the example of Brazil, which despite facing severe objections from the addicted structures of power, the media, parliament, and judiciary, has advanced and can no longer go back, because its people won't accept any more ideological regimes that delay the nation, bring ignorance to the people, finance countries with the same ideology encouraging corruption, and the diversion of public resources.

The digital economy is the way, and Crypto-economy is the new science of this digital economy, where technology dictates the rules of an increasingly, decentralized, not intermediated and distributed market, with less state, but private initiative, fewer intermediaries and regulations and more self-regulation, less government, more people, and a considerable increase in Peer-to-Peer relationships (person to person), reducing costs, simplifying processes and drastically reducing the final value of an asset, product or service.

Author Contact:

Marcus Lisboa

Email: mvla2015@gmail.com / inepp@inepp.org.br /

eco.finances@principautedeseborga.com

Twiter: @Marcus_Lisboa38 - @interesseP

Parler: @MarcusLisboa   - @InteressePublico

Instagram: @marcusvlisboa - @doutorblockchain -

@interessepublicoBrasil

https://conservativecore.net/MarcusLisboa

Facebook: https://www.facebook.com/marcusvlisboa/

Linkedin: https://www.linkedin.com/in/bitsblockchain/

Site: www.marcuslisboa.com.br

www.inepp.org.br

www.popblockchain.com

www.cryptotech.com.br